D1488078

# The River Home

Also by Franklin Burroughs

Billy Watson's Croker Sack

# Franklin Burroughs

# The River Home

## A Return to the
## Carolina Low Country

Illustrations by John M. Bryan

Houghton Mifflin Company Boston New York

The text of this book is composed in Weiss,
with the display set in Antique Roman and Antique Open.
Composition by the Maple-Vail Book Manufacturing Group.

Library of Congress Cataloging-in-Publication Data
Burroughs, Franklin.
[Horry and the Waccamaw]
The river home : a return to the Carolina low country / Franklin
Burroughs ; illustrations by John M. Bryan.
p.    cm.
Originally published: Horry and the Waccamaw. 1st ed. New York :
Norton, © 1992.
Includes bibliographical references.
ISBN 0-395-64382-1 (pbk.)
1. Waccamaw River (N.C. and S.C.) — Description and travel.
2. Canoes and canoeing — Waccamaw River (N.C. and S.C.)   3. Horry
County (S.C.) — Description and travel.   4. Burroughs, Franklin —
Journeys — Waccamaw River (N.C. and S.C.)   5. Burroughs family.
I. Title.
[F277.W33B87   1993]
917.57'87 — dc20            93-12163
CIP

Printed in the United States of America

AGM 10 9 8 7 6 5 4 3 2 1

Previously published in hardcover by W. W. Norton & Company, Inc.
under the title Horry and the Waccamaw.

To the several generations, again.

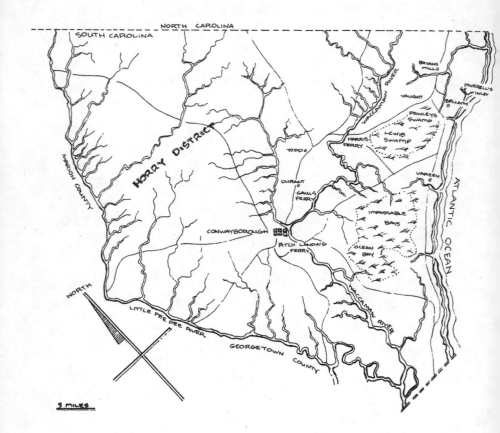

# Acknowledgments

I am particularly indebted to the Horry County Historical Society, upon whose publicaton, *The Independent Republic Quarterly*, I have drawn very heavily. Also, for permission to quote from *The South Carolina Rice Plantation* (Chicago) and *A Woman Rice Planter* (Harvard).

Professor Charles Joyner, of the University of South Carolina at Myrtle Beach, has provided encouragement, and, in his own work, the example of a historiography which is local in focus but not in implication.

# Contents

# The River Home

# 1    The Independent Republic

Historically, Horry* County, South Carolina, remains unapproachable. There exists a map of it from 1820. The fact is that the county is roughly diamond-shaped, its northern boundary, which is the North Carolina line, slanting diagonally down from northwest to southeast, its eastern boundary—the Atlantic Ocean— sloping from north northeast to south southwest. But the mapmaker of 1820 rotated the whole county counterclockwise by 45 degrees, so that the arrow indicating true north points to the upper left-hand corner of the map instead of pointing straight up. He no doubt did this to fit things more efficiently onto a rectangular piece of paper; in doing so, he created a geographical design that looks approximately like a reversed image of the Iberian peninsula. The northern boundary becomes a straight line running east-west; the Atlantic coast, like the coast of Portugal, runs north-

---

*Pronounced Ō-RĒĒ. The pronunciation, which is obviously French, has thus far survived the orthography, which looks English. Peter Horry, an aide to Frances Marion during the Revolutionary War, was of Huguenot extraction. I have been unable to determine the original spelling of his name. *D'Orée*, literally meaning *from the margin of a forest or river*, would be phonetically plausible, and, given the county's long history as a marginal sort of place, poetically appropriate.

3

south. Answering to the long Mediterranean coast of Spain, as it runs from Catalonia down to Gibraltar, is the Lumber River, which comes down out of North Carolina, joins the Little Pee Dee, and forms the western and southwestern border of the county. From Gibraltar, the Iberian coast turns northwest, toward Cádiz and Portugal. Horry achieves the same configuration by rather complicated means—the boundary follows the Little Pee Dee to its confluence with the Big Pee Dee, but then, instead of following the Big Pee Dee on downstream, the county line jogs east northeast through Bull Creek to the Waccamaw. It continues a short way down the Waccamaw, then goes overland, northeastward across the narrow peninsula of Waccamaw Neck to the Atlantic.

If you look at a map with any degree of curiosity, you speculate about the logic of boundaries. Rivers, oceans, and mountain ranges are self-explanatory and so not especially interesting. What is interesting is a boundary that has no obvious topographical justification, as is the case in southeastern Horry. Studying the map, you wonder why the line didn't continue on down the Pee Dee a few more miles, until it emptied into Winyah Bay. Or why, having missed that chance, and gone through Bull Creek to the Waccamaw, it didn't follow the Waccamaw down to the Bay. Why put a surveyor to the trouble and expense of running a short line, of no more than five or six miles, northeastward across Waccamaw Neck?

The map of 1820 notes that the whole of Horry County lies "within the alluvial formation." Few citizens of the county would have understood what that meant, and fewer would have assented to the geohistorical assumptions behind it: for them, Horry County, like the rest of the world, lay within the post-diluvian dispensation, and that was that. But elsewhere, the map uses a vocabulary that, while perfectly understood in Horry and surrounding counties, might confuse outlanders. There are, for example, several lakes named on the map, but the bodies of water in question are clearly minor tributaries of the Waccamaw and Pee Dee. More

4

numerous and, to the uninitiated, more puzzling, are the bays, unconnected to any ocean, sea, or lake, which the cartographer has scattered throughout the county—a large one lies to the east of Conwayborough, for example, and is labelled simply "impassable bay." Such bays are wet, dense thickets; they may have a scattering of stunted cypress and pond pine, but their primary vegetation is the sweet bay, an evergreen, glossy-leaved shrub that is closely related to the magnolia.

The map shows a few roads—one running along the coast and one paralleling the Pee Dee form a perimeter, from which perhaps a dozen roads in all lead into the center of the county, eventually to meet at Conwayborough. Conwayborough is the only town, and it lies just to the south of the center of Horry, at the mouth of Kingston Lake, the longest of the Waccamaw tributaries. Elsewhere, the cartographer has simply put the names of individual farmers, and occasionally indicated a schoolhouse, church, or mill, suggestive of some sort of rudimentary community. The names are English, Scotch-Irish, and Huguenot: Bryan, Jordan, McRacken, Vaught, Vereen, Durant, Bellamy, Beaty, Tillman, Brown. These remained common names in the county when I was growing up there in the 1950s, and many of them were still prevalent in the same sections where the mapmaker had found them in 1820. They had of course been augmented by other names—Jolly, Mishoe, Chestnut, Parker, Long, Causey, Spivey, Jenrette, Smith, Watson—but these appear to have the same provenance as the ones on the map, and had been in the area for a long time.

Rivers, swamps, and bays isolated the county. Roads were primitive at best, and altogether impassable at high water. The Pee Dee swamps rendered communication to the west and southwest difficult, and there was only one inlet—Little River, just below the North Carolina line—that afforded anything like a harbor, and it would have been a shallow and precarious one. The rest of the county's forty or so miles of coastline consisted of broad, sandy beaches, broken occasionally by tidal creeks, locally known as

5

swashes. This coastline is distinguished, along the eastern shore of the United States, by its complete absence of barrier islands. The sea rolls directly in to it, and I am qualified to say that landing an outboard skiff, or anything much larger than a surfboard, is a tricky business, even on a balmy summer afternoon. But had the coast been more inviting, there still would have been problems getting to the interior. "Impenetrable bays" and the swamps of the Waccamaw River, which runs roughly parallel to the coast and about ten miles inland, formed a second line of defense. In the deep geological past, the coastal strip had been a barrier island, and the Waccamaw had been the sound that sundered it from the mainland; in the nineteenth century, although no longer an island, the coast remained effectively insulated from the rest of the country.

In Europe, where civilizations evolved slowly and had established themselves firmly before the advent of the industrial revolution, it is still possible to remind yourself that, for most of our history, topography has been destiny. The elevations of the land, the navigability of the rivers, the configuration of the coast, the arability of the soil were all givens, and history had to work around them, respecting and variously reflecting them in cities, boundaries, and nationalities, in local customs, dialects, and styles of architecture. The role of topography in American history is generally less obvious—the present, with its enormous powers of obliteration, can negate the constraints, obstacles, and with them, the opportunities that inhere in local geography. It renders the past invisible, and in many ways renders geography invisible, too. This is especially true within the alluvial formation, where geographical change is so subtle as to be almost imperceptible to a traveller travelling in the usual way—in a car that devours the miles of long, flat road running through a country of small farms and pine woods, occasionally dipping slightly down to a causeway that carries it through a swamp, and perhaps over a shorter or a longer bridge, which registers as a momentary change in the pitch and rhythm of the tires' humming, and is past almost before the image of dark, lazily winding water has had time to impress itself.

The early, obscure history of the country was determined by a topographical fact so slight that even a pedestrian would not notice it, and that could be measured in inches. The lower reaches of the Pee Dee and Waccamaw rivers had enough tidal range, and swamps that were extensive enough, to permit the growing of rice on a vast scale. Those reaches all lie within Georgetown County; the county line, wandering from the Pee Dee through Bull Creek to the Waccamaw, and thence to the coast, had a logic that would have been immediately apparent to anyone travelling by boat up either the Waccamaw or the Pee Dee at any time prior to the Civil War. Below the county line, the traveller would have encountered mile after mile of diked fields, flooded or drained, depending upon the season, and would have seen, on the west side of the Pee Dee and the east side of the Waccamaw, a succession of plantations—the more or less imposing planters' houses, the "streets," or quarters, of slaves, the array of outbuildings, including, perhaps, a mill, that made each plantation into a small village. Above the line he would have seen no more ricefields, and few signs of more than isolated, individual human effort of any sort.

For as long as topography had much to say about it, Horry County was destined to be a backwater. A grim index to economic development in antebellum South Carolina exists in the statistics of slavery. The census of 1850 counts 25,563 slaveholders in the state. Of these, barely 1 percent—257 to be exact—lived in Horry. And of these 257, nearly a quarter owned only a single slave, and more than half owned fewer than 5 slaves. The contrast to Georgetown County is extreme. In 1850, a total of 5,522 white people in Horry County owned a total of 2,075 slaves; in Georgetown County, 2,193 whites owned 18,253 slaves. While slaves were used in a great variety of ways, their primary use was as farm machinery, and Horry, so deficient in something so essential to commercial agriculture, was *ipso facto* limited to a subsis-

7

tence economy. Investment did not go there; reliable roads, bridges, and markets were not established. A certain amount of money was spent, from time to time, in clearing the rivers of snags and sandbars, but neither the Waccamaw nor the Pee Dee was an artery of commerce. Rafts of logs came down them to sawmills on the lower river; sometimes the rafts also carried turpentine, tar, and resin, to be shipped from Georgetown to points north and east. But very little went back up the river, and that little was mostly staples, of the sort that might be supplied to a frontier town or wilderness trading post. The county's history began like the history of almost every settlement along the Atlantic seaboard; the difference was that it simply did not evolve, or evolved only minimally, neither making history nor participating in it. Its population remained small—geographically the largest county in South Carolina, it was also the least populated, until the very end of the nineteenth century.

The antebellum South was of course full of pockets like this, and the inhabitants of such places, long before the Civil War, had become stereotypes—backwoodsmen, piney-wood folk, white trash, po'buckras, dirt-eaters, corn-crackers, red-necks. An open or implied contempt for them is the only social attitude that seems to have generally been shared by abolitionists, slaves, and slaveowners, and their stock did not go up appreciably after the Civil War. As a class, they generated no image of themselves to oppose the stereotypes that opposed them, no cultural evidence of the human significance of their heritage. Success for them involved the betrayal or denial of their origins, requiring them to become planters or merchants or bankers. Even the politicians they elected typically represented them to the world with a certain kind of blustering buffoonery and exaggerated coarseness, as though unable to take themselves, or their constituents, with much seriousness.

Georgetown, which had been fired upon by British guns during the Revolution, was only forty miles from Conway; Francis Marion, the Swamp Fox, had operated out of the Pee Dee swamps

8

against Tarleton's supply lines. Stephen Foster's song had originally been "Way down Upon the Pee Dee River"; the Suwannee was later substituted for reasons of mere euphony. Ninety miles from Conway was Charleston, with its long, eventful, and emphatically unforgotten past. But armies, artists, and famous personages boycotted Horry—it was unsung, unworthy an invader's attention, and is today surprisingly empty of even the humblest sorts of antiquities. Despite the fact that the same people have lived in the same places for so many years, there are remarkably few churches, houses, or barns that antedate the twentieth century. Local memory has no shrines. In junior high school, we all studied South Carolina history for a year, and we learned absolutely nothing about Horry that we could not have seen for ourselves—that it was a large county chiefly given to the production of tobacco, timber, and pulpwood. The county had picked up the nickname of "the Independent Republic" somewhere along the line, but its independence seems to have been a good deal like the chastity that so many of us endured all through high school—a virtue not much tested by opportunity.

Opportunity eventually came, and the Independent Republic went the way of Malkyn's maidenhead. By the time I left the county in 1960, things were beginning to change rapidly, and now when I return there, I find a place that seems to have seceded from its own history, and joined the gung-ho, synthetic, commercial culture of the sunbelt. The effect has been overwhelming along the coast, where the dunes have disappeared under high-rise condominiums, and where 9 or 10 million tourists visit annually. Inland, change is less spectacular, but it is real. Small farms are dying out; agribusiness has arrived. This had not involved depopulation, however, because the countryside is for the first time being inhabited by large numbers of people who do not farm, but who live there because the towns and beaches are overflowing. Between 1980 and 1986, Horry's permanent population increased by 26 percent, and that was good enough, or bad enough, to win it thirteenth place in the national growth sweepstakes, in which every county with a population of more than 100,000 was entered. Small parcels of land, suitable for residential construction, are said to double in value every four years. At last count, there were something more than forty golf courses in the county. These and other statistics come blaring in from every side; local pride at last has something to celebrate: "real estate brokers easily recall instances where an oceanfront lot costing $45,000 in 1966 has been sold for $300,000 in 1985. That is an increase of 567% in just 18 years. One of the more interesting accounts involves an oceanfront lot that cost $7,000 in 1953, which was sold for $150,000 in 1980. Since that date, the lot has been sold for $185,000, providing a total increase of 2,543% over 30 years." The topography that had been so resistant to improvement in the nineteenth century now seems infinitely malleable, and in danger of disappearing altogether. A college campus, a golf course, industrial parks, shopping malls, automobile dealerships, and any number of residential developments fill the "impassable bay" that separated Conway from Myrtle Beach. Tidal marshes have simply disappeared; "jerseyfication"—wind and water erosion caused by building on the duneline—has drastically diminished the "Grand Strand"—the long, unbroken beach that stretches from North Carolina to Winyah Bay.

A modest attempt at cultural salvage was begun in Conway in 1966, with the establishment of the Horry County Historical Society. It publishes *The Independent Republic Quarterly*, holds meetings, sponsors occasional outings to spots of historical interest, and has opened a small museum in the old post office building on Main Street. It is an uphill battle. The county's history is undramatic and, until the twentieth century, undocumented. The huge influx of outsiders and money has not helped—it drowns out the indigenous accent, dislocates the families whose long continuance in one place was the essence of the county's history and its substitute for an articulate tradition, and it introduces a point of view that is not inclined to celebrate a past characterized by isolation (a nineteenth-century traveller observed that farms were so scattered that each had to be serviced by its own tomcat), poverty (one estimate puts per capita income in 1895 at $2.50 per annum), and, in a variety of respects, ignorance ("There are people in this county today," writes Van Norton, a Conway lawyer, in 1908, "well off in this world's goods, skillful in business, clear-thinking, square men, who cannot, or barely can, sign their names." Norton also found the county to possess a certain kind of *idiot savant*, especially when it came to politics: "There are men who can read you Greek like a dog a-trotting who know no more of the selection of a proper officer for constable than a wild man from Carver's Bay or Catfish. 'Vote for the politest man' is as good a rule as he can give you. The man who can't read and write at all, and don't think, will himself almost invariably give you this rule in one way or another.") The *Quarterly* relies very largely on reminiscences by older citizens of the county, which are supplemented by old letters, old newspaper articles, wills, court records, and rarely by a more formally researched and written essay on a particular topic. It does not impose any uniform standards of historiography or prose composition upon these materials, and the effect of reading through a pile of *Quarterlies* is about like sifting through family relics in the attic, or listening to old people talk. It is often tedious, trivial, and aimless, and you need to suppress your own self-important notions of consequentiality to attend to it, but that is about the only way to begin to develop some feeling for life in a place where so little seems to have happened.

Our own ideas of individual consequence are themselves consequences of an idea of history. Thoreau would not have been Thoreau if he had lived along the Waccamaw. When he went down the Concord and up the Merrimack in 1839, he could see the rivers as they were and, with very little effort at research, as they had been. He could draw from Johnson's *Wonder-Working Providence* to describe the river meadows of the Concord as they

11

had appeared two hundred years earlier, could recite Emerson's hymn as he rowed past the "still visible abutments" of the North Bridge, refer ichthyological questions to Josselyn's *New England Rarities* (1672), and use a merchant's Day Book from 1805, showing the purchases of a fisherman between March 25 and June 5, at which latter date the account is suddenly settled, to speculate that herring, shad, and salmon must have appeared in the river in late May, rendering the fisherman temporarily solvent. But there were no Puritans to carry into Horry an exalted consciousness of historical mission, and, if the figure about per capita income in 1895 is even close to being right, precious little reason for a merchant to keep a Day Book. In his survey of Horry politics, Van Norton (a writer, I might add, of much pungent good sense—"the only cure for bad politics is more politics") pointed to an excess of independence as the overriding fact of county history:

> We are lacking in social solidarity—the organized community cohesion that adds so much to individual success, and that makes individual success worth so much more to the community. We have need consciously to strengthen that mutual aid in social development and enlightenment, the facts of which are hard to define, but the effect of which is so easy to see and feel in the life around us.

Social and historical consciousness, without which there is small likelihood of any articulate individual consciousness, does not flourish in a subsistence economy, on scattered farmsteads serviced by a tomcat in residence.

Judging from what the Historical Society has found so far, no one in Horry felt important enough to keep an elaborate diary or maintain and preserve an extensive correspondence. At best, there are genealogies in family Bibles, with perhaps a brief memoir written for the grandchildren. Some of these are unexpectedly powerful, beyond any intention the writer could have had. They remind you of what history is at its source—men and women, their hard, unevolving struggle against life nearly over, finally confronting the unfamiliar recalcitrance of the written word, trying to leave some testament:

> Heare is a rekerd of the pipel of the fambly Smith put doun as best I no as fer bak as I can rekol. When I am ded I want one of my sons to rite en what he nos and pas it on afor he dies so enothr can pik it on up. I dont no no more then who my pa ware and his kin an them now stel livin. I wil put doun like in the bible. Heare it is to be kep as long as fambly and time gos on by. I start. . . .
> Now it loks like this is what I no. I am gittin ohl and tird my helth is not good. My wife Ella died a time bak I hav mised her but I am heare with Bill [his second son] an wold not wont to be no othir place. I am redy to go when the tim gits heare. I leve this rekord fer my relations as I have no money or land to give.
> I sine mi name

John N. Smith
May 1884

The impression you get from the *Quarterly* is corroborated by the historical museum. Its chief exhibits are tools, harnesses, a logging cart, a few distillery bottles, a wood stove—the sort of thing you might expect to find in an old barn. These are supplemented by some models, illustrating, for example, the manufacture of tar and turpentine, and a few relics of the aboriginal Mississippian Indians—shards of pottery and arrowheads. One is struck by the poverty and simplicity of the material culture of all three races—red, white, and black—that had inhabited the area. Except for the pottery and the arrowheads, most of the objects in the museum continued to be in use within living memory—the memory, that is, of my father's generation. But looked at now, they seem artifacts out of a primitive past, whose rudimentary technology would have been familiar to the earliest European settlers in North America.

Of course local history need not rely entirely on indigenous materials. The eighteenth and nineteenth centuries saw many travellers to and through the South, and some of these left more or less famous accounts of their journeys. But none of the famous ones ventured into Horry. Audubon missed it. The actress Fanny Kemble, who wrote memorably of her short, unhappy life as the mistress of a Georgia sea-island plantation, came overland from Philadelphia to Wilmington, North Carolina, just forty miles above Horry. But, having passed judgment on Wilmington ("a place I could sooner die than live in—ruinous, yet not old—poor, dirty, and mean, and unvenerable in its poverty and decay") she took a steamer to Charleston. Frederick Law Olmsted, that most observant and determined of travellers, also came to Wilmington, took a steamboat up the Cape Fear River, and made his way by rail and stage down through Marion and Kingstree, keeping to the west of the Pee Dee swamps, and seeing nothing of the territory that lay between them and the Atlantic. Even Sherman found nothing in this poor place to tempt him, and stayed to the west, and so did the Civil War in general. (All the reasons that kept travellers and armies out of Horry brought large numbers of Confederate deserters into it in the final months of the war, and they operated as brigands, stealing whatever they could find. This led to the county's only military engagement, when a group of citizens in Conway organized to oppose these desperados and succeeded in killing one of their own number, John R. Beaty, mistaken for a deserter by one of his fellow militiamen in the thick swamps to the east of town.) Coming down on a fact-finding mission after the war, J. R. Dennett (*The South as It Is, 1865–66*) followed Olmsted's route through Marion and Kingstree, described what he heard and saw in those places, and left Horry to its usual oblivion.

Of the very few travellers who entered the county and left any account of it, the most notable was James Robert Gilmore (1822– 1903). Gilmore was a man of some significance: a native of Massachusetts who moved to New York, made enough money there to retire while still young, and to devote the rest of his life to literature and politics, which were two names for the same thing. He was a prominent abolitionist, an ally of Horace Greely; he wrote for the *New York Tribune*, and co-founded and edited *The Continental Monthly*, an important anti-slavery magazine; he served as an unofficial emissary in a curious peace overture from Lincoln to Jefferson Davis in 1864; he later wrote the campaign biography of James Garfield. But what mattered to me was that, shortly before the Civil War, he had visited the household of a Colonel J——, who had extensive holdings in the pineland of northeastern Horry, where he produced turpentine, tar, and pitch. Gilmore's account of that visit is found in a book called *Among the Pines*, which he published under the pseudonym of Edmund Kirke in 1862.

I ran across references to *Among the Pines* in the *Quarterly*, located a copy, and sat down to read it with great eagerness. And it did afford me the strange pleasure of seeing names like "Waccamaw" and "Conway" in an old book by a professional writer, and of correlating the Horry County he encountered—a forbidding, exotic, and dangerous-sounding place—to places that were so ordinary, so familiar that I had never looked at them or considered what threat or promise they might once have held. I could identify most of the people he met: his Captain B—— was certainly Henry Buck, a transplanted Yankee who had established a large sawmill on the lower Waccamaw; his Colonel A—— was either J. Motte or Benjamin Allston. And his host, Colonel J——, could only be Colonel D. W. Jordan, a North Carolinian who had moved into upper Horry in 1848, acquired land along the Waccamaw, and, within a decade, had made himself a rich man. Gilmore credits him with 20,000 acres and 270 slaves; historical evidence suggests that the actual numbers were about half that, but the exaggeration does not distort the nature and extent of Jordan's operation.

You must admire and envy a writer who went so far upstream from civilization, to seek out a hidden place full of Conradian possibility. But Gilmore, despite his assurances that every event and conversation in his work is "verbatim et literatim *TRUE*, and

15

was taken down . . . within 24 hours of its occurrence," wrote much that was literally and demonstrably untrue. He tells us that he visited Jordan in the winter of 1860–61, but by that time Jordan had sold his acreage in Horry, and purchased and moved to Laurel Hill, a rice plantation on the lower Waccamaw, in Georgetown County. In a postscript, Gilmore describes the gallant death of the Colonel, leading this troops into battle near Roanoke, Virginia; Jordan was in fact too old for active service (his title was purely honorary) and was an unhappy and querulous survivor of the war and its aftermath.

Inaccuracies of this kind don't necessarily signify; there is more to truth than fact. But Gilmore's book is full of contrived implausibility, the least of which is an alligator swimming in the Waccamaw River in January. In the two weeks of his visit, he learns of a highly sophisticated revolutionary organization, unknown to any white man but himself, that exists among the slaves of the Waccamaw and Pee Dee basins. He discovers that the woman who is to all appearances Jordan's wife is in fact his octoroon mistress, and that Jim, a slave, is Jordan's half-brother. He witnesses a murder (Moye, the lecherous white overseer, kills Sam, a slave), a double suicide (Julie, Sam's wife, takes their child in her arms and walks into the Waccamaw), a narrowly averted fratricide (the Colonel and Jim), an escape and a thrilling, if unsuccessful, pursuit (Moye, on the Colonel's best horse, eludes the Colonel and Gilmore), a tornado, a barbeque, a political rally, and a revival, all occurring in the depths of a gloomy wilderness. Twice the impetuous Colonel is on the brink of fighting more or less incidental duels with his po' white neighbors, who are either slovenly, illiterate, and secessionist, or thrifty, industrious, and Unionist.

The limitation of Gilmore's book had nothing to do with his convictions, which were, after all, shared by the best observers of the antebellum South, Frederick Olmsted and Fanny Kemble. His problem was that he was not a witness but a propagandist, and a strangely uningratiating one. *The Dictionary of National Biography* speaks of the "rather flatulent self-satisfaction" of his literary persona, and that seems to me exactly right. The remoteness of Horry, the undoubted ignorance of its inhabitants, and the moral horror of slavery all served him as backdrop, against which he manipulated melodramatic situations and stereotypes, and exhibited to maximum advantage his own complacent blend of worldly sophistication, unflappable coolness, and irreproachable rectitude of political sentiment. The Librarian of Congress, whom one does not envy, decided to list his book under the following headings: 1. U.S. South—Social Life and Customs; 2. U.S. History—Civil War; 3. Fiction.

I found myself reading the *Quarterly*, visiting the museum, leafing through nineteenth-century American travel literature, and hardly knowing why. Both of my parents, and most of my remoter ancestors, had lived all their lives in the county, either in Conway or northeast of it, further up the Waccamaw or over by Little River, but this did not distinguish us from most of the people we knew, and nobody attached any importance to it. I had experienced no particular wrenching when it came time to leave and live elsewhere—if I had grown up in a world where people went on living in the same place generation after generation, I grew into one where it was calmly accepted, if not expected, that you would follow your career, and go where it took you.

Years later, I came upon George Eliot's celebration of the notion of a home place, a homestead:

A human life, I think, should be well rooted in some spot of native land, where it may get the love of tender kinship for the face of the earth, for the labors men go forth to, for the sounds and accents that haunt it, for whatever will give that early home a familiar, unmistakable difference amidst the future widening of knowledge: a spot where the definiteness of early memories may be inwrought with affection, and kindly acquaintance with all neighbors, even to

dogs and donkeys, may spread not by sentimental effort and reflection, but as a sweet habit of the blood.

This of course was a warning against the centrifugal and abstract-
ing forces of the nineteenth century, against a widening of knowledge that had the effect of deracinating its possessors, cutting
them off from the indispensable, concrete reminders of our final
dependency upon the earth and what it nourishes. I trust that no
one who has encountered Eliot's passage in *Daniel Deronda*, or who
encounters it here for the first time, can read it without some
reference to his own life, her own life. I think that most of us feel
the force of its propositions, although we may never have experienced the reality it describes.

It seemed to me, as I thought about it, that although Conway
and the county were still there, they were, for most of the people
now living in them, much less particular and peculiar than they
had been—there was less and less of anything that could be called
"a familiar, unmistakable difference" about the places themselves,
the labors that people went forth to, or the accent they spoke. I
was not interested in the issue of whether what had been gained—
a higher standard of living, a greater diversity and tolerance, a
"widening of knowledge"—outweighed what had disappeared.
History and memory were suddenly becoming important in Horry
County, where they had never been so before. It was the old
consolation claimed for people living obscurely in one place that,
when they died, they would pass into the landscape that was
everything they knew, and that the landscape, absorbing each
generation in its turn, and only slightly modified by the labors of
that generation, would serve as a visible and outward memory for
the generations that followed, carrying within itself the labors of
the ancestors, which would shape, in quite definite ways, the lives
of the descendants. But now all that is reversed, and, in Horry
County and most other parts of the globe, we outlive our landscapes, and must tell our children Elysian tales of the groves and

18

fields and marshes that underlie parking lots. In Horry, circumstances delayed for a long time any real awakening to this fact; oral, familial traditions sufficed, because the continuities of local history, and of the undramatic landscape that was its chief monument, were so much stronger than the discontinuities. But that is no longer true. The accumulated memory is disappearing with the landscape, and people can no longer assume that, simply by being born in the county, they have its history by heart, and need not think further about it.

About ten years ago, on Cape Cod, I wandered into a used bookstore and, looking for nothing in particular, picked up a volume called *On the River*, edited by M. W. Teller. It was an anthology of canoe and small boat voyages, most of them undertaken in a spirit of genteel adventure and more or less elegantly recorded. They dated from the nineteenth and early twentieth centuries, and except for the obligatory bit of Thoreau, none of the essays was familiar to me. I bought the book and eventually read it. The second essayist, after Thoreau, is Nathaniel Holmes Bishop, who had written book-length accounts of two long voyages he had taken in the 1870s—the first, in a canoe, down the Atlantic coast to Florida and there, via the St. Mary's and Suwannee rivers, to the Gulf of Mexico; the second, in a gunning skiff, down the Ohio and Mississippi to the Gulf. Teller included excerpts from both books, with the editorial observation that Bishop is a writer who deserves to be better known. But what struck me more than Bishop's merits as a writer and hardihood as a boatman, was a casual observation he makes near the end of his canoe trip, on the St. Mary's River in Florida: "Swamps have their peculiar features. Those of the Waccamaw were indeed desolate, while the swamps of the St. Mary's were full of sunshine for the traveller."

And so it appeared that, when he reached the long, open shore that stretches from the North Carolina line to Georgetown, Bishop had gone inland, and made his way down the Waccamaw. Teller's anthology included nothing from that portion of the trip, so I set about finding Bishop's book, *The Voyage of the Paper Canoe*, which was published in 1878, and has not been reprinted since. This took a little doing, but I eventually got access to a copy. Although my interest was parochial and specific, it was impossible not to read the book from start to finish. Bishop had begun in Quebec City, ascended the St. Lawrence to its junction with the Richelieu, gone up the Richelieu to Lake Champlain and from there, via canal, into the Hudson and so on down to the Atlantic. His canoe—a light wooden frame covered with heavy manila paper treated with a special marine glue—was made by E. Waters and Sons, of Troy, New York, and represented a state of the boat-builder's art that I had never heard of. It was tiny—fourteen feet long, only twenty-eight inches in beam, and nine inches deep at the center thwart—and it weighed fifty-eight pounds. It had oarlocks mounted on steel outriggers, and could be rowed or paddled. When paddling, Bishop sat amidships, and used a double-bladed kayak paddle. He travelled light and trusted a good deal to the hospitality of the people he met along the way. His narrative suggests a man whose modesty was as unself-conscious as his intrepidity and resourcefulness.

When he got down the coast as far as Wilmington, North Carolina, he placed his little boat on a baggage car and went thirty-two miles by rail to Lake Waccamaw, the source of the Waccamaw River. I sat in Maine and read his account of the trip down the Waccamaw—150 miles in all—and it seemed to me that I should retrace this part of his journey. I knew the Waccamaw for perhaps 70 of its miles—40 miles above Conway and 30 miles below—and there were blank stretches even in that portion. And I knew no one who was familiar with the upper third of the river, where it was reputedly narrow, shallow, and frequently obstructed by fallen trees. So I waited for the chance, and, in late March of 1985, drove south with my canoe, an 18-foot Old Town guide model, of traditional wood-canvas construction, built in 1960 and bought secondhand by me in 1968, the year I moved to Maine. It is 36 inches amidships, 14 inches deep at the center thwart, and weighs 100 pounds. I had recanvassed it in 1984, at the end of the summer, renewed the varnish, recaned the seats, and put new "rails"—gunwales—on it. They were of good, clear New England ash—the original ones were Philippine mahogany—and the blond, strong-grained wood, contrasting to the green of the hull, made the canoe better than new. Bishop was a forward-looking man, and travelled in a boat that, in the basic idea of its design—the reliance on a rigid, molded skin unsupported by ribs and planking—looked ahead to the aluminum, fiberglass, royalex, and kevlar canoes of the present day. In comparison to it, the Old Town was an unadventurous boat, of retrospective design, and well suited to my purposes.

# 2 Lake Waccamaw to Freelands

On a bleak Sunday morning with a northeast wind driving a fine, misty rain into the windshield, Daddy and I headed up from Conway toward Lake Waccamaw. The first twenty miles were through familiar territory, but when we got beyond Highway 9, which runs from west to east and crosses the Waccamaw at Bellamy's Landing, we entered what was for me almost a new country, although it ought not to have been. My mother's father had been born here, in the small community of Buck's Creek, on the west side of the Waccamaw, and had found his wife in Little River, a few miles to the east. But he was upwardly mobile, moved to Conway, and left Buck's Creek and Little River emphatically behind him. My mother and her sisters and brothers do not seem to have consorted much with their country cousins, and I became aware of this group of relations only as they died, at which time my sister and I would be put into our least inhabitable clothes and, on some unendurable summer day, be driven over roads that shimmered in the heat until they seemed to float above themselves in an asphalt mirage. We would eventually arrive at Buck's Creek or Nixon's Crossroads or Little River, and there be introduced to any number of Bryans and Stones and Vereens and Vaughts, all of whom made a collective, blurred impression of awkward diffidence, a lack of the fluency and self-possession I expected of grownups. The service would be Baptist, and entirely without the sanctified impersonality of the Episcopalian disposal of the dead. To me at that time, accustomed as I was to the archaic remoteness of *The Book of Common Prayer*, it all seemed a poor show, insufficiently distinguished from the earnest and fumbling sincerity of ordinary life.

So now we drove on through Buck's Creek and toward North Carolina. This part of the county seemed untouched by all the changes that had taken place; it was still a region of small farms, with an occasional church or crossroads store. I had no topographical maps, and had to make do with two road maps, one of Horry and one of Columbus County, North Carolina. As we passed into North Carolina, subtle differences became apparent. We were leaving behind the pattern of gentle undulation typical of most of Horry County, with sandy ridges falling off gradually to bays, branches, and swamps, and entering a flatter, more sparsely populated country. The farms were smaller and fewer, the fields as flat as runways, and the black soil here looked heavy and impermeable, like clotted mud. The roadside ditches had a fine growth of cattails, indicating that water stood in them year round. It felt as through we were going into a lower and lower country as we went further and further upriver, but that of course was not possible. In an alluvial terrain, distance above sea-level is not what counts; what counts is distance above swamp level. The swamps around Lake Waccamaw, which we were now entering, are on average about forty feet above sea-level; those around Conway are about half that. But the high land around Conway may be twenty or thirty feet above the level of the swamps, while here such high land as there was would be only three or four feet above the swamp. We were at the southern edge of Green Swamp; the stretches of ground high enough for farming and human habita-

23

tion are labelled on old maps as islands, and some of them still go by that name: Sweetgum Island, Pine Island, Clifton Island. These were originally savannahs, forested with longleaf and loblolly pine, and now they sustained a few meagre farms.

Because I had no adequate maps, we decided to turn east at Pireway, North Carolina, and cross the river, continue up it for a few miles on that side, and then re-cross at Freeland. That would give me at least two points of reference, some way of measuring my progress down from Lake Waccamaw.

The river at Pireway was unexpectedly broad—perhaps seventy yards across—and there was a landing on the east bank, just downstream of the bridge. My first impression was of a row of cars and pick-ups there, neatly parked and glistening incongruously between the dark, rain-dimpled surface of the river and the gray trunks of cypress and gum rising from the swamp behind them. We were already in the middle of the bridge before we realized that there was a baptism in progress at the river's edge. Forty or fifty people stood in a semicircle in front of the cars and trucks, facing the river. Their attention was focussed on the minister, who stood in shallow water, flanked by a young man and a young woman. These three, facing the congregation, had their backs to us, but we could see that the minister was reading from a big Bible that he held up in both hands, his head and shoulders tilted back to balance the weight of the book.

I slowed down and stopped, trying to take it in—the lowering skies, the skeins of Spanish moss moving softly in the wind, this solemn gathering by the river. Our normally acute sense of sabbath-day propriety deserted us entirely, and I think we would have sat parked on the bridge, gawking as rudely as any tourists, had not several somber faces in the congregation lifted to look at us, and the minister, by a slight twisting of his neck, indicated that he was aware of our presence. It was enough to show me what we were—two men in a truck, with Yankee license plates and a canoe on top, stopping to stare. I put the truck into gear and slunk on across the bridge, still watching out of the corner of my eye. My last view was of the faces turned back to the minister, and of the black current as it eddied around his knees, pulling at the severe crease of his pant legs, and at the waterlogged hem of the young woman's dress.

We drove on and talked about this and that. The rain would pick up for a moment, then relent; the windshield wipers kept up their steady rhythm of polish and smear, polish and smear. Although the hardwoods were at the point of unfurling into leaf, the flat land did not look hopeful. The clouds hung low and unbroken, it was chilly, and one had the sense of seed rotting in the drowned furrows. Daddy spoke practically of what a cold christening the two young people by the river were in for, when time came to wade out deeper—waist deep, maybe—and be dunked down below the surface. Often, he said, when a young woman was being baptized, her mother would sew lead battens into the hem of her skirt, so that it would not imperil anybody's modesty by floating up around her hips as she stepped into deeper water.

I asked if he had ever seen a Waccamaw baptism before, and he said he had once, just after the war. On a Sunday morning he and his brother Jack, a merchant in town, had put in at Red Bluff and run upriver to fish the Little Savannah territory. The war, like every war, had had the effect of undermining local pieties: before it, fishing was permissible in salt water on Sunday, but not in fresh water, unless it was your own private pond. Sunday hunting was unthinkable. This was not a matter of law—game laws in Horry County were generally regarded as a challenge, not an inhibition—but a matter of decency. After the war, people began to fish in the river on Sunday—at least townspeople did—although they did so somewhat self-consciously, as Jack and Daddy had that morning. Unsanctified or otherwise, they caught enough fish, cranked up the fine new Martin outboard motor, and headed back to the landing. Jack was at the tiller, and Daddy said that when they rounded the corner above Red Bluff he had two simultaneous perceptions—one of a crowd of people looking a good deal like a herd of cattle at a watering hole, and the other of the little Lumberton boat heeling over so sharply that he had to grab the gunwales, and heading back upstream and out of sight. Jack had a lot of regular customers in the Red Bluff vicinity. He and Daddy tied the boat to a piling upriver, sat on the bank, and waited out the service, until at last the congregation dispersed, and they could slip back to the landing unobserved, load the boat, and get home to a cold Sunday dinner.

We re-crossed the river at Freelands. It was small here, not twenty yards wide, and I was happy to see a good sandbar downstream, which meant that the water was low enough to furnish me plenty of campsites. Then we continued north to the lumbering town of Hallsboro, turned back east, and reached Lake Waccamaw not long before noon.

A kind of expectation, based on obvious metaphors, attaches to sources and headwaters. I knew almost nothing about Lake Waccamaw. A natural lake of any sort was a rarity in the Carolinas, and this one was further distinguished by the huge swamp that surrounded it. It has long attracted speculative interest, of one sort or another, although nobody seems to have taken much interest in the river that flowed out of it. Both of the botanical

Bartrams went there. In July of 1765, John Bartram found slaves building tar-kilns to the east of the lake, and was characteristically delighted by "the great variety of lovely plants & flowers & in generally the finest lofty pines I ever saw" that grew on the savannahs, or "islands," that lay to the north. But "the so. west is very swampy. The outlet is at the so. end into the Wocoma river which runs a course of 50 mile & most of the way very stil water." He found fossilized shells, but had little conception of the extent of geological time: "it must be long ago when the sea flowed here: for the lake is now very fresh & produceth now the fresh water mussel as all our rivers do." His son William came there eight years later, describing it as "the beautiful Lake Wakamaw, which is the source of the fine river of that name [that] runs a south course of seventy or eighty miles, delivering its waters into Winyaw Bay at Georgetown." He deemed the "vast rich swamps" to the northwest of the lake, "fit for the production of rice" and his sense that, if only the swamps could be cleared and drained, they would provide the basis for a prosperous and sustainable agriculture, remained alive throughout the nineteenth century. But nothing substantial was done until the twentieth century, and then it was the logging industry, and not agricultural interests, that began digging canals, building causeways, and slowly diminishing the Waccamaw watershed.

But on this Sunday morning, Lake Waccamaw, seen from the county road that runs along its western shore, was a disappointment. The shore was low, scarcely a foot above water, and as perfectly flat as the lake itself. It was lined with summer houses, each house basically a box on stilts at the water's edge, and each with a dock extending a hundred feet or so out into the lake. Each dock had a boatshed at the end, and a big outboard runabout suspended from the rafters of the shed, so that the effect was of coming upon a lake where all the boats had gone to roost. There were no people about—it would be a few weekends yet before smoke from the charcoal grills would waft along the waterfront

27

and the boats and water skiers would buzz round and round, like waterbugs in a birdbath. The Lake itself, approximately round and about six miles across, looked immense in the light mizzle of rain. The wind had raised a chop on it; nothing about it suggested depth or lucidity.

The county map showed something called Waccamaw State Park, located at the end of the road and just beside the outlet. It turned out to be an exercise in minimalism, consisting of a fifty-five-gallon oil drum placed at the end of the sandy little road, and an unimproved landing. There was a certain amount of sodden garbage in the drum, and considerably more—wrappers, styrofoam cartons, bottles, cans, and other familiar excrescences of a vigorous and diversified economy—scattered around the landing. We stopped and got out and looked at the Waccamaw River, separated from Lake Waccamaw by a low concrete dam, over which there flowed an inch or two of water. The river spread out into the swamp, but a main channel was distinct. It looked like any little branch or creek near Conway—Crabtree Creek or Sterrit Swamp or Smith Lake: somewhat sluggish, quickly losing itself among the second-growth gum and cypress, in the lower branches of which was caught more undegradable junk—aluminum cans and plastic bottles and vaguely obscene streamers of cellophane.

After we had put the canoe in and before we loaded it, Daddy suggested that it might be well to paddle a little way downstream, to be sure that the river was passable. This was in part a sensible precaution, but I thought it also likely that he wanted to see at least a small stretch of the headwaters of a river upon which he had, over the course of seven decades, spent so many hours. And so we launched out, experiencing again the initial, and mostly illusory, sense of precariousness and hazard that you get when you step into a canoe after being landlocked for the winter. The stream took a couple of sharp turns; we ducked under a big water oak that had blown over, and made a bridge of itself, and under sagging, black-barked grape vines, some of them as thick as a man's thigh, and then came to a second oak, this one lying too low across the stream to duck under. We could see where a boat had been dragged around its upper end, and so got out, walked over a short, miry portage, and looked downstream. The river was clear as far as we could see, which was about two canoe-lengths. "Well, do you want to go ahead with it?" I thought so, although it looked like there would be a lot of portaging, of packing and unpacking the canoe. I had half expected that, and had my gear pretty well consolidated into a single pack and two waterproof plywood boxes. So we returned to the landing, loaded the canoe, and said goodbye. Daddy said he would wait at the landing for half an hour, in case things got bad enough downstream for me to change my mind, and go back down to Freeland and put in there. "Just yell," he said. "From the looks of what we saw, it'll take you all afternoon to get out of earshot."

I reached the portage and carried over the gear and the canoe, nervously timing myself as I did so. Seven minutes—at that rate, I could be spending more time afoot than afloat this afternoon. Within two turns, there was another tree, its crown fallen squarely into the center of the stream. But when I got to it, I found that half a dozen limbs on the underside of the trunk had been sawed off, making just enough room for me to squeeze through. The cuts were made with a chainsaw, and it seemed strange to me that a passage had been made here but not on the upstream tree. Both trees were uprooted, and both lay in the same direction, as though victims of the same storm. But I was glad to profit from this ameliorated windfall, and gladder when it became apparent, within the next hundred yards, that the sawyer had continued on downstream. He was obviously a thrifty man in a small boat. The openings he cut were narrow, and it usually took a certain amount of tugging and prying to get the canoe through, but I never had to portage again.

Except for the saw cuts and, for the first mile or so, an occasional soda bottle or hamburger carton, there was impressively

scant evidence of man. The forest—red maple, water and laurel oak, tupelo and black gum—had, like all the Southern woods, been logged more than once, but not recently. Big, dark grapevines were everywhere, crisscrossing the understory of the swamp and hanging low across the stream. I went what I estimated to be three miles without seeing anything that distinguished itself in any way; I might have been going in a circle. I wished that my botany were better—as was the case everywhere in the low country, there were a good many trees, and a great many shrubs, that I did not know, and so had no way of recognizing what might be distinctive about this swamp. There is a real consolation, an antidote to isolation, in being able to name by their right names all the things that surround you, and I could not do that here. There were many young red maples, their pale gray bark splotched and stippled with white, and their winged seeds, brilliantly red, hanging in thick clusters; but apart from them, the swamps of the Waccamaw were, as Bishop had reported them, indeed desolate.

The rain had suspended, but the raw east wind was steady.

There were few signs of life. From time to time a pair of wood duck would flush ahead of me; their squealing made a large commotion in this still and silent place. The one telling observation I was capable of making was that the high-water mark, indicated by bands of pollen and the upward limit of a shaggy, brownish-green moss on the trunks of trees, was less than six inches above the stream, although the stream itself, after a dry spring, was not high. This was an indication of the vast size of the swamp I was in—in time of freshet, the water could spread out horizontally for miles, and so rose very little. At present, the floor of the swamp was out of the water, although you would stop short of calling it dry land. It was dank and oozing, and when I had made my one portage, each footprint had filled immediatly with water. I had about four more hours of daylight, and began to get a little uneasy about finding a place to camp. In the swamps around Conway, you could count on the occasional hummock, and these would normally be indicated by one or two big loblolly pines, which do not like wet feet, but which seem to colonize any little elevation in a swamp, no matter how remote. So I looked sharp through the treetops, hoping to see pines, but there was nothing.

I went around one tight bend after another, pulled under fallen trees, and then went around one more corner and there, silent and sudden, was more sky that I had seen since Lake Waccamaw, and, on creosoted pilings, a one-lane bridge, so low that I would have to duck going under it. The road that crossed it was sand, with a very thin layer of tar on top, and last year's dead weeds sticking up through every crack and break in the tar. After the closeness of the swamp, it had a slightly unreal quality, like a low-budget hallucination, and this quality did not vanish when I pulled in against the bridge and stood up, and looked both ways, up the road and down the road. Judging from the weeds, no traffic had passed this way since at least last summer. The bridge looked new—the creosote was still black and glistening, and the trusses had not begun to sag and settle. It was undoubtedly a logging road of recent construction, but it seemed peculiar that there should be no sign of traffic—log roads are built for immediate use, and are used until they are used up. This one was a riddle, and it added to the afternoon's feeling of emptiness and abandonment.

But it would at least be a dry place to camp, if not a very inviting one. I checked my watch and decided to paddle for another hour. If I had found nothing better by then, I could return and sleep on the low causeway, or the bridge itself, without much risk of getting run over. Below the bridge, the river re-entered the obscurity of the swamp, and so did I, but with a certain expectancy now.

Two bends downstream, I saw something gleaming ahead of me in the swamp, by the edge of the stream. Seen first through a screen of vines and branches, it had an unnatural radiance, like fox-fire or phosphorescence, yet it resolved itself, as I drew around the corner and saw it clearly, into nothing more than a stack of lumber—to be more precise, a stack of ten-foot cypress rails. They looked like the sort of split rails that are used for suburban fencing when a rustic effect is desired, or by the coupon-clipping gentlemen farmers of the Shenandoah Valley. But these rails had been sawed with a chain saw. The sawyer had taken some trouble to make them wedge-shaped and irregular in cross-section, so that, from even a short distance, they looked like they had been split with a maul and wedges. Looking into the swamp behind the rail-pile, I could see a scattering of sawdust on the dark leaf-mold, and the stump of the cypress, and the trodden ground where the man had worked. The pile of rails would have amounted to something less than half a cord of wood—a good day's work. The neatness of the pile, stacked tightly between two young maples, was impressive, and so was the degree of trust or isolation it implied— in Horry County, anything left unlocked beside the river in the morning would be circulating in the local economy by midafternoon. Or at least that would have been the case in my boyhood but—who knows?—perhaps the denizens of the Waccamaw had

32

at last become the self-respecting, godfearing, and trustworthy yeomen of American legend.

But what impressed me most was simply the odd lambency of the new-cut wood, which contrasted strongly with the muted grays of the living trees that surrounded it. The cypress was tawny in color toward the center, shading out to the pallor of sapwood beneath the bark. Its brightness was mirrored and doubled by its reflection in the black water, where, wavering in the slow whorls and eddies of the current, it seemed to issue continuously out of itself, and continuously to disappear, like flame. It was strange to see all this and yet know that it was only a pile of wood, and that, whether left here or taken to fence in somebody's yard or hog-lot, it would soon weather to the neutral tone of ordinary lumber.

Soon after this, the river opened up into a long straight stretch, twenty-five or thirty yards wide. For the first time, I could see whole trees reflected in the water, and not just overhanging branches. The swamp was slightly lower here, and the trees stood in shallow water. But off to the east, obscured by the intervening treetops but still unmistakable, I could see the crowns of pines. Closer at hand, almost every cypress that stood out into the river had a trotline suspended from one of its low branches. There were also, at wide intervals and in no discernible pattern, plastic bottles anchored in the stream, serving as buoys of some sort, but I could not guess their purpose, and when I tried to pull one up, it didn't budge.

As I reached the end of the straight stretch, there was a sudden commotion in the swamp to my right, a great thrashing and splashing, and I stood up in the canoe just in time to catch the quickest glimpse of the white tails of two deer. If the canoe had startled them, their own noisy flight seemed to give them the illusion of a pursuer, and their frantic plunging continued for as long as they were in earshot. When I sat back down and looked ahead, there was a big water oak across the stream, and a sluggish flow of water passing into the swamp around the upper end of the oak. My sawyer had not touched this one, which seemed to indicate that I should work my way around the upper end, through the swamp, and back into the river on the other side. But within a few yards, the flow of water played out, and lost itself, and me, in the swamp.

I had gotten out and dragged the canoe some distance, in water not much deeper than the rubber bottoms of my boots, looking back to the right all the while, in every expectation of seeing open water in that direction, when I heard the buzz of an outboard motor ahead of me and to the left. It drew toward me and passed, invisible through the trees, but causing a fractional surging and then a faint subsidence in the water at my feet. Even allowing for an overcast day, an unreliable sense of direction, and the featureless confusion of a swamp, it made no sense at all, and there was nothing to do but drag the canoe back out the way I had come, and reconsider the river.

By the time I got back to open water, the outboard had faded on out of hearing upstream. It might have been the trotliner, I thought. I paddled upstream a short distance and there, to the east, was what was unmistakably the outlet, exiting from the side, rather than the end, of the long straightaway. It must have been at about this point that I had flushed the deer on the opposite bank, and, attending to them, had missed the outlet. As I turned into it, I heard the whine of the outboard, coming back downstream, and in a few minutes an aluminum johnboat came skimming toward me. It contained a man, at the tiller, and two girls. Because I was close in against the bank, they were nearly on me before they saw me and the man turned quickly to shut the motor down, and the boat settled abruptly into the water, wallowing for a moment in its own wake.

"Well where'd *you* come from?" he asked, and I set about explaining, with considerable embarrassment, how I'd happened to be out of sight when he had come by before. He looked doubtful, but then said for me just to follow him, and I couldn't go wrong. He asked if I'd had any trouble getting down this far, and I told him no, that everything had been smooth sailing, because somebody had cleared out the channel enough. "I done that," he said, "and you might notice I left one right there below the lake. Don't want all them big boys on Lake Waccamaw coming down here. Anybody can paddle, I'm glad to see 'em. I live right round the corner here, not quarter-mile away. You stop by, and stretch your legs a little." I thanked him and told him I would, and he cranked up and, putting ahead of me at barely more than paddling speed, led me down the stream, then up a short dredged-out channel to his house.

"This here is my daughter and her friend," he said with a nod in their direction as I got out. "They been after me to take 'em ridin' in the boat, so we was just out ridin'." The two girls, shy and friendly both, gave me quick, ducking nods and a bright laugh, and skipped up to the house. I tried to take in my host, and his house, and a strange little boat, half full of water, that was tied to a cypress-knee beside us. We shook hands, and he told me his name was Thomas Spivey, and that they all lived here, himself and his Daddy and Mama and his wife and daughter, and that he didn't ask anything more.

He looked to be in his middle thirties, of about average height, but of much more than average trimness and tautness. Everything about him was cleanly and pleasingly weathered. His face was brown, square, and well creased around the eyes, and his hair evoked Hollywood's idea of what a backwoodsman ought to look like—black as a horse's mane, long, and combed straight back. His hat, the style of a hunter's hat with a narrow brim that turns up in back, was made of cotton, and it had originally been brightly patterned with the trademarks of the most popular American beers— the kind of cheap hat sold mostly to high school boys who hope to be mistaken for hard-drinking college boys at Myrtle Beach or Surfside. But the hat had faded out almost to whiteness, with only the faintest traces of the colorful designs left in it, and hooked in its narrow band were a dozen or so small bass bugs, that were definitely not ornaments—the enamelled paint on them was cracked, and you would say that their tail feathers and rubber legs were much the worse for wear, except that any kind of fishing lure is always much the better for wear, which is the proof of of its efficacy. His shirt at the shoulders was as bleached out as the hat; you had to look down a way to see that it was a gray workshirt, worn to the softness of flannel. He wore blue jeans, all the stiffness and most of the dye gone out of them too, and his boots, despite the muddy landing where we stood, were newly oiled and clean.

He saw me looking at the boat at our feet. It was, with very slight modification, the aboriginal design of the whole region, and indeed of all naval architecture in any part of the globe where good-sized trees grew in convenient proximity to the water. Compared to it, my canoe, and the bark canoes that inspired it, were newfangled high-tech gimcrackery. "That's a old-timey log boat," he said. "I dug it for my Daddy." I had seen specimens of such boats in museums, and they had been fairly common on the river in my father's youth, but this was the first one I had ever seen in a state of nature. It was unmistakably primitive, with the slightly lumpy, imperfectly symmetrical quality of something made from modelling clay. I asked Thomas about it, and he told me to come on up to his shop, he was working on one there.

The shop, standing between his house and the river, turned out to be a shed, and a rough shed at that—a pieced together tin roof that looked like it had been salvaged from an old tobacco barn, supported on cypress poles that stood, erratically braced and trussed, directly on the ground. There were no walls and no floor, just the slick, trodden earth and a few planks nailed between the poles to provide a work table and a place for tools. In a pile of tawny chips on the ground lay the new log boat, almost complete. It was ten feet long and not quite thirty inches wide—slightly smaller than the one at the landing. The boat was bluntly double-ended and flat-bottomed, with the bottom rising noticeably as it narrowed toward the bow and stern. Its sides had only a slight flare—most of the rotundity of the log had been cut away. Inside, it was gouged out to a depth of about ten inches. There was no seat, but this boat, like the one at the landing, had a fish box—two partitions, or bulkheads, of log had been left, about a foot apart, in the middle of the boat, and the space between them had been dug out and two half-inch holes drilled through the bottom. A cypress lid was fitted over the fish box; the hinges which held it, and the nails which held the little cypress decks at each end of the boat, were the only hardware involved.

It began raining again while we were under the shed—"I'm going to put me some hot-top up there this summer, fix her up nice," Thomas said, by way of comment on a good many leaks—and so we stood and talked for a while. He showed me his tools, which were basically a foot-adze and a hand-adze, which he called a howel. Both were wickedly sharp, but otherwise they looked more closely related to agricultural implements—a hoe and trowel, say— than to anything you would expect to find in a craftsman's shop. He took a piece of scrap plank and demonstrated the foot-adze. The handle was long enough for him to stand almost erect, with the board under his forward foot. The blade came into the wood a few inches ahead of his big toe. With a few neat strokes, he dug a groove in the plank, one that would compare favorably with what a weekend carpenter could do with a mallet and chisel—the depth of the cut was uniform, the edges clean and straight, and the bottom nearly smooth. The howel had a short, curved blade, and he worked it with a quick flipping motion of the wrist to shape and smooth the wood until its surface looked almost as though it had been planed.

I asked him about the various things I had seen coming down. The rails were his: "Fence-railing. Sell all of it I can make. But it's hard to find cypress anywhere. Sometime I find a old log about half buried out in the swamp. Might have been there a hundred

year, and still sound as a dollar. I hook up a come-along to a tree and snake it out that way. Them bottles up there in the straight-away? They mark a couple old logs sunk in the river. This summer when she gets down real low I'll get 'em out. I make all kind of things out of cypress—benches, swings, fenceposts."

What he most liked to make were the boats, but it took an unusually fine piece of cypress to make one, and that drastically limited his production. The one in the shed was already bespoken by a doctor in Tennessee, who would pay him two thousand dollars for it. "That seems like a lot of money, but what people don't realize is, there ain't much cypress left." He did other things too: trapped some in the winter—raccoons, bobcats, otters, and mink—and caught snakes in the summer. He had sometimes worked as a dragline operator and swamper for Georgia Pacific—"That bridge you come under? I done that, working right by myself. It was so you could drive clear acrost to Hallsboro, but there was that bridge an a nother one, and some of them boys over on the Hallsboro side got mad at G. P. about something, and burnt the tother one down. So the road don't go nowhere now"—but he preferred making a living on his own, here at the edge of the swamp. "If you do good work, and garntee it, your name'll travel. I been on tele-vision three time, showin' how I build my boats and catch snakes.

Now I can't keep up with what folks want to buy. I had a man to write me from Fairbank, Alaska, asking about log boats. But I tell you this—I don't care how many folks want it or how fast they want it, when I build a thing I build it right, and if it ain't right I fix it or buy it back. I ain't got nothin' but my name in this world, and folks will tell you about Thomas Spivey, when he does a thing, he does it right."

The rain had stopped again, and he showed me around. He kept his snakes in a low, reassuringly well-built cage of hardware cloth. At present there was only one—"They ain't out good yet, and this early one that is out is like to be so poor he'll die on you, but this is a right good one for this time of the year"—a moccasin of about thirty inches, tightly coiled under a small watering trough inside the crate. He sold the snakes to universities for research and the production of antivenom. Almost any snake has some value, but moccasins were the silk of the trade, and he pursued them from the Virginia line all the way down to Georgia, living out of his pick-up truck, hunting them at night with a spotlight in the hot weather.

Beyond the cage was a greenhouse, built very much like the workshed, with juniper posts and dirt floors, but enclosed in builder's plastic. Here I met his father, who was transplanting seedling tomatoes from various sytrofoam containers—cups, boxes, hamburger cartons—that looked as though they might have drifted down from Waccamaw State Park. Mr. Spivey's hair was nearly white, and he was a good deal stockier than his son. Like his son, he treated me as though I were doing him a favor by interrupting his afternoon—"Ain't a thing I'm doing here can't wait"—and he told me about his greenhouse. He had always liked to farm some, but had reached the point where he couldn't do it any more, and a few years ago Thomas had built him the greenhouse. "Daddy done good out of it," said Thomas. "Made us right proud." He raised mostly vegetables, with a few flowers and houseplants, and sold them locally, to neighbors who were too busy to bother with a vegetable plot, but still liked the taste of fresh tomatoes in the spring, or a good bunch of collards. "It took some money to build," said Mr. Spivey; "they don't give that plastic away. But I told Thomas when we built it: 'We ain't got nothing so we ain't got nothing to lose.' You can't lose nothing if you ain't got nothing, and you can't get nothing without you lose something. We didn't inherit nothing but our name, and a man's name ought to be enough. It's been enough for us."

Much of what he said had this somewhat oracular quality, and he spoke with a deep placidity. Thomas listened respectfully, saying little, but plainly agreeing with his father. "It was me taught Thomas how to dig a log boat, and I never see anybody to do a better job of it. He built that one down there at the landing, and give it to his Mama and me as a gift. I want you to paddle that boat before you leave. His Mama and me go fishing ever day, if the water ain't froze over. It froze right over this winter: temperature of zero degree, plus the wind chill. But otherwise, if it ain't froze or Sunday, we go right out ever day. Cold weather, we take and put a lard stand right on the fishbox, build us a little fire in it." I asked him what they caught, and he called the fish by names I had not heard for a long time—morgans and goggleyes and bonnet brim; jackfish and stumpknockers and redfin pike.

I did not go into the house. Like the other buildings, it was low, did not appear very sturdy, and seemed to incorporate a good deal of recycled material. It looked like something casually improvised out of whatever was handy. It occurred to me that the average middle-class American, seeing such an establishment in passing, would probably express a degree of indignation, either against the people who were willing to live there, or the society which reduced them to it. But talking with the Spiveys was a great antidote to this sort of reaction; I felt no tendency to wish other circumstances upon them. They had been here, on this bit of highland in the swamp (which is named, rather *too* appropriately, but there it was, right on the Columbus County roadmap: Crusoe

Island) since way back, Mr. Spivey told me. From all appearances, his remark about nobody inheriting anything was strictly accurate: there was nothing in this ancestral homestead that would have been as old as Thomas Spivey himself, and nothing that seemed likely to outlast him. In the cluttered, grassless yard, and the makeshift style of the architecture, there was more than a suggestion of life on a frontier, or an extended bivouac. It contrasted strongly with the neatness, enterprise, and skill of the two men themselves.

Northern travellers in the South, throughout the nineteenth century, commented upon the squalor and primitiveness in which most rural whites of the non-slave-owning sort lived; the contrast to the thrifty and tidy farmsteads of New England or Pennsylvania was irresistible. Houses of unchinked logs, mud and stick chimneys, unglazed windows, and dirt floors seem to have been common, and even more prosperous dwellings struck outsiders as lacking rudimentary amenities. Buildings, and indeed the material culture in general, made no statements, affirmed no traditions. The Spivey house belonged to a regional idiom of architecture that was neither traditional nor contemporary in aspiration. It was purely extemporary, improvised to provide shelter, and not a great deal more, against a generally mild climate. It was not pleasant to imagine an August night in one of its small rooms, with the air thick with mosquitoes from the swamp and dank with mold and mildew. But it seemed clear that Thomas Spivey preferred this way of life—a man who could operate a dragline and build bridges as solid and neat as the one upstream could command a respectable salary, and live in an FHA-approved house: for that matter, he could build it himself.

I was torn between wanting to stay and talk and needing to get on downriver before the rain resumed or darkness fell. We said goodbye to Mr. Spivey and walked back toward the shed. As we passed Thomas's truck, there was a strange grunting and growling from beneath it, and then a dog emerged: a fyce bitch, obviously

41

old and fat as a woodtick. She ambled gravely up to Thomas to get patted. He scratched her ear, and pointed to her back, which was rumpled and greasy: "She 'bout lives under that truck; likes to hump her back against the pan and get oil all over it. Helps keep off the fleas. She's a smart dog. Fourteen year old and still the best squirrel dog you'd ever want. She'll eat anything, though—only dog I ever see that'll eat tomatoes, right off the vine." She rolled over on her back, and Thomas gave her an affectionate pat on the stomach. "You ain't exactly perishing to death, is you?" he said to her, and we walked on. The little dog lay on her back, her fore-paws limply aloft, peering after us, and seemed to give some thought to getting up and following us, but decided against it, sighed, and settled down to a nap.

When we stepped back into the shed to get a paddle, Thomas showed me more of his handiwork, stashed under a tarp and wait-ing to be sold. It was all strongly and simply made—a crib that, with the addition of a lid, could have doubled as a rabbit hutch; some shallow wooden bowls, of the sort that are used for knead-ing bread; a milking stool. These things were truly rustic, and belonged here, but they were not destined to stay here. They would be sold in shops along the highway between Wilmington and Myrtle Beach, along with suntan lotion, beach towels, fire-crackers, darkglasses, and T-shirts that announced their wearers' willingness to cross state lines for immoral purposes. Some of the work was done on commission. There was a section from the bole of a hollow cypress, three feet long and standing on one end, with a little raised roof, below which was a crude crank, on the other end. "That's a wishing well. Lady in Charlotte asked me to make one for her last year. Now her sister's got to have one." There was no trace of irony or amusement in his voice. Next to the well were two benches, which looked like the next thing the lady in Char-lotte might buy, to get back ahead of her sister. They were not the kind of product you would associate with any self-respecting craftsman, and could be forgiven only if you saw them as a gleeful

exploitation of our enormous, uninformed nostalgia. But Thomas
Spivey did not see them so.

Mr. Spivey's log boat was too heavy—about four hundred
pounds, Thomas reckoned—to pull up and tip over, so we bailed
it with a scoop. I expected it to be tippy—I had had some experience with little one-man fishing boats, made from planks, plywood, or cypress strips, that were of its size and general design.
But this one hardly seemed to notice when I stepped in and sat
cross-legged on the floor. The bows were raised enough so that
the boat did not plough through the water; once under way, it
moved along easily, and held a steady course. I paddled up the
dragline cut to the river, turned, and came back. Thomas then
took the boat, to show me some things about it. One was its
stability; he could stand comfortably on the back deck of the little
boat, or paddle it from the fishbox—its weight kept the center of
gravity low. He had an easy, loose-jointed way of being in a boat,
his legs folded under him, the paddle, no longer than a pizza
spatula and with a considerably narrower blade, managed with
one hand.

It was time to go sure enough, although I felt reluctant. I asked
him if he would sell me one of the wooden kneading bowls, and
he consented. We dickered for a while over the price—I wanted
to pay him the retail price, which was low enough, but he insisted
on wholesale. The bowl was a pretty thing, the howel marks still
visible in the pale, almost grainless wood. "That's tupelo," he said.
"Only thing to make a bowl out of. My uncle, he's took to makin'
'em now, and he'll just make 'em out of anything; juniper or sweetgum or maple. Me and him's had some discussions about that; we
don't get on so good. Your tupelo won't never warp or check on
you; them others will." I thanked him for everything and shook
his hand and got back into the canoe. As I stashed my new pos-
session into the pack, he said for me just to keep it dry till I got
home, and then to rub some cooking oil into it. "Do that, and
every couple years rub a little more oil in, and she won't never

give you no trouble. I garntee it to last. You bring it back if it don't."

As I resumed my trip downriver, I thought about the log boat, and its merits in a place like this. Thomas Spivey had had nothing good to say about canoes. He considered them noisy, hard to manage in a wind, and, as he put it, *slippery*—"You stand up in one and it's gone right out from under you." For his purposes, the log boat *was* better. Deep in the water, it moved as quietly as an alligator. When you are fishing along the river bank, moving with the current and casting in toward the bank, stealth is everything and speed is nothing. A wood canvas canoe, paddled slowly, is one of the quietest things I know, but there is a slight slapping noise associated with its progress and, when moving under minimum power, it is susceptible to any gust of wind, which forces you to do a certain amount of bracing and prying with the paddle. The log boat kept you low; you nudged it along with only the slightest twist and flex of the wrist. Paddling it, Thomas had seemed to merge with the slow deliberations of the river, and the muted backdrop of the swamp. It belonged here, where its design was as indigenous and functional as that of the cypress tree itself. I wondered about the doctor in Tennessee, soon to be the owner of the boat back in Thomas's shed, and I hoped that he lived over in the western part of the state, and had some bayou or swamp for it, and would know how to use it. But I suspected that the odds were against it; there were not many people of means who still did the kind of unsophisticated, yet highly skilled, fishing and hunting for which this boat was intended.

I passed several hummocks high and dry enough for camping, and each was prominently posted by Georgia Pacific. Despite Thomas's assurance, I felt a little skittish about pitching my tent directly under a sign that forbade my doing so, and so kept paddling and hoping for less forbidden earth. I was soon regretting it: the hummocks came further and further apart, and the darkness settled rapidly—once the sun has gone below the horizon, light

44

fails quickly in a swamp. There was still light in the sky, but almost none at ground level, when I heard a car door slam, an engine start, and had a glimpse of headlights as the car pulled away. From the Columbus County map, I knew that this had to be Old Dock, where a county road crossed the Waccamaw. I found a narrow strip of dry woodland between the road and the river, and pulled ashore there, pitched my tent, and cooked and ate my supper in the last gloom.

It was a poor place I had chosen. The strip of woods had been recently cut, and heaps of slash and bulldozed stumps surrounded me. Beside the highway, right at the edge of the river, were three of the big iron dumpsters that are now used for rural trash collection. This, in the abstract, certainly represents a real and useful progress over the traditional way people had of getting rid of their refuse—by dumping it on somebody else's land, ideally that of a paper company or an absentee owner. But considered concretely and at close range, the dumpsters were smelly, sordid, and, as the hours wore on, increasingly noisy with the rustling and scuffing and squealing and growling of raccoons and rats. I'd might as well have pitched my tent in a back alley of Hoboken. It was a restless, wretched, interminable night. I read some, by the light of a candle lantern. I had at the last moment realized that I'd not packed a book, and so had taken an old copy of Rousseau's *Confessions* from my parents' bookshelf. I'd thought it might be just right, a book offering neither forward impetus nor any particular resistance. But Rousseau did me no good; I read his misunderstood life in the same irritated, impatient way that you read magazines in a dentist's office. It occurred to me that this was not the first time I had found that you couldn't cheat insomnia by boring it to death.

Bad as it was, my night was better than the one Bishop spent in this vicinity. He had "shot into the whirling current which rushes out of the lake through a narrow aperture into a great and dismal swamp" at about noon, with a letter in his pocket from Mr. Carroll, his host at Lake Waccamaw, to Mr. Hall, who operated a turpentine still at old Dock. Bishop normally rowed, but the Waccamaw, "this most crooked of rivers" obliged him to use his paddle, so that he could face forward. His prose, normally well-pruned and vigorous, develops a certain entropic luxuriance in the depths of Green Swamp:

> Down the tortuous, black, rolling current went the paper canoe, with a giant forest covering the great swamp and screening me from the light of day. The swamps were submerged, and as the water poured out of the thickets into the river it would shoot across the land from one bend to another, presenting in places the mystifying spectacle of water running upstream, but not up an inclined plane. Festoons of gray Spanish moss hung from the weird limbs of monster trees, giving a funereal aspect to the gloomy forest, while the owls hooted as though it were night. The creamy, wax-like berries of the mistletoe gave a Druidical aspect to the woods, for this parasite grew upon the branches of many trees.

He got to old Dock—obviously somewhat further downstream than my present location—late in the day, and found a scene of industry and enterprise. Rafts of logs blocked the river, and on a sandy bank, surrounded by pines, was the turpentine distillery, sending out smoke and resinous steam. Mr. Hall occupied a two-room shanty—one room with a table and a fireplace, the other with a double bed. Hall told Bishop that he had been sent out from Wilmington to oversee the still and manage the "turpentine farm," which consisted of four thousand acres of pineland, valued at five thousand dollars. He found the job lonely, and was glad to have a visitor.

But as they prepared for bed, there was a great shouting outside, and one Jim Gore, thoroughly drunk, barged in. He was a justice of the peace, the local embodiment of Law and Decency, and as such was immediately mistrustful of Bishop, whom he apparently took for some kind of spy. Bishop, who seems to have

46

been a tactful and disarming man, eventually won him rather further over than was comfortable, and found himself being tearfully embraced by Gore, and warned of what lay ahead: "O stranger, my heart is with ye; but O, how ye will have to take it when ye go past those awful wretches to-morrow; how they will give it to ye! They most knocked me off my raft, last time I went to Georgetown. Beware of them; I warn ye in time. Dern the hussies." Bishop understood this to be a reference to "rough women," and was full of alarm, imagining that something about like furies or maenads lay in store for him downriver; it was not until the following day that he realized that Gore had meant *reaches*, long, windy stretches of open water.

Gore insisted that he must share the bed with Hall and Bishop, and share it he did. Bishop spent the night crammed against the wall; Hall spent most of it on the floor; and Gore slept the sleep of the blest, or at least the drunk, there in the middle of the bed. Rousseau, or any other purely metaphoric bedfellow, ought to have seemed pretty tolerable by comparison, since he could always be shut up and put aside. But restlessness to the night, like evil to the day, seldom leaves you with any sense of its insufficiency, and I stumbled out of the tent at the first diffusion of darkness, made coffee, ate, broke camp, and left, feeling weary even before I reached whatever reaches or wretches the day might bring.

But the sky began to clear. A red-shouldered hawk cried out to the east and soon circled into sight, haloed in the early sun above the shadows of the swamp. On the first corner below my campsite, a pair of wood-duck swam out from among river birches and sat eyeing me. The drake cocked his matchless head, tensed, but did not fly. Furtively, like a pantomime of eloping lovers, he and the hen sank low into the water and, making no ripple, slipped back toward the trees at the river's edge. Thomas Spivey had told me that they were not nesting yet, but were almost entirely paired off, and that I could tell which ones had already picked out a nesting tree because they would, like these two, be quite stubborn

in their refusal to leave its vicinity. Whenever a normally shy creature, for whatever reason, permits you a long, breathless look at itself, you are for that moment admitted to a sanctuary, and everything goes quiet and still inside. I set the paddle across the gunwales and drifted; drops fell from the blade; the hawk cried again. The hen disappeared back into the birches, but the drake, his neck extended forward and low to the water, still watched, fiercely vigilant over his small life, until the current had taken me around the corner and out of sight. These events, the hawk and the wood-duck, established something that lasted for the next three days, until I turned up Kingston Lake and came back into Conway. At almost any time I listened for it, I would hear the bluejay's voice of a red-shouldered hawk, and I was to see, between Old Dock and Conway, exactly 126 wood-duck, or about one pair every half hour. In the same stretch of time, I would meet three other boats and have five conversations, four of them perfunctory.

That was all to come. I passed under the bridge at Old Dock—a momentary, creosote-dank and resonating darkness—and then back into the morning light. Just downstream from the bridge were inviting pine woods on the east bank, perhaps descended from the turpentine farm. That industry left few traces of itself; it seems to have been figuratively, as well as literally, a cut and run operation, like so many economic undertakings in this part of the world. I hoped I might see an old chimney or some other bit of brickwork remaining—everything else would be rusted and rotted back to nothing—but saw only the pines, their crowns a yellowy green in the shafts of early sun.

The day was bright but cool, and I felt this morning a stiffness I would not feel again. The next bridge was at Freelands; judging from the Columbus County map, it would not be far below Old Dock. But I came to yet another prostrate oak—with their heavy-branched crowns and shallow roots, the swamp oaks seemed to have a greater horizontal propensity than other trees—and this one completely thwarted the river. If my canoe had been made of one of the new, bulletproof synthetic materials, I could have dragged it across the trunk, but since it wasn't, there was nothing for it but the bucksaw. It took fifteen minutes of awkward labor to cut away enough of the crown to force my way through, with much rasping and scraping of branches. A few bends further on, two more oaks had fallen, from opposite sides of the stream. Neither extended all the way across the current, and one was about ten yards down river from the other. In even moderate white water, this would have been a very difficult and dangerous problem, but on the smoothly pulsing current of the Waccamaw, it wasn't worth the second thought I didn't give it, as I slipped around the first tree, turned unhurriedly above the second, and started across current. It is important to my self-respect to invoke, at this point, a sudden, capricious, wholly unanticipatable gust of wind, to account for my finding myself being borne down into the crown of the second oak. I ducked under a branch; it caught solidly, like a mast in a mast-step, in the downturned hood of my parka, shoving me almost out of the canoe, which rolled enough to take water. It would have been a cold christening on a Monday morning, but I managed, by blind and frantic groping, to catch the limb behind my head and push away from it until the branch came free. That turned out to be my last obstacle on the river, and I had an inch of water sloshing in the bottom of the canoe as a souvenir.

The map notwithstanding, it was a long way to Freeland. The river was serpentine and the serpent was coiled. I had not quite understood how Bishop could have found himself paddling down stream, but up current; but I could understand it now. On a small-scale map, the Waccamaw runs approximately south-southwest from Lake Waccamaw to Georgetown. On a somewhat larger scale map, you can see that it makes a shallow, backward-facing S— flowing southeast until shortly below the South Carolina line, then swinging back the other way, reaching its westernmost point near Conway. It looks straightforward and simple, with that appearance of unconfused motivation which we attribute to life in an earlier age of history, or to people whom we do not know well. But the moral of the river was that there is always room for deviation, even within the confines of a straight and comparatively narrow fluvial corridor. I set my compass atop a plywood wanigan, and watched it until I grew deliberately dizzy. Within a mile, I had gone through this sequence of bearings: S; SSW; SW; WSW; W; WNW; NW; NNW; N; NNE; NE. When I reached the NE reading, it was apparent to me that I would soon come to an overpass, which would enable the river to cross itself and carry out some plan it had conceived last summer for estivating in New England, or that I would go backward through the same set of readings I had just registered. The current continued to go my way, but, if the river had been high enough to flow overland through the swamps, I, like Bishop, would have been obliged to paddle upstream, as well as directly away from my eventual destination, in order to get where the river was going. Its insinuations spoke for a devious fatality: you might have to buck the current in order to follow it, and turn back toward your point of departure in order to reach your conclusion.

I had plenty of time to formulate these morals and chew on

50

them. Bishop had left Old Dock with Gore's enigmatic warning of wretches and hussies ringing in his ears, and also with practical advice from Hall: "Keep to the main stream, though it be more crooked and longer. If you take to the cut-offs, you may get into passages that will lead you off into the swamps and into interior bayous, from which you will never emerge. Men have starved to death in such places." I saw any number of places where the river ran strongly out into the swamp, and they gave every appearance of being cross-country expressways, but I observed Mr. Hall's admonition scrupulously, and passed them up. Finally, at one of them I took careful note of a big dead cypress some distance in— a single limb jutted out to the right of the decapitated trunk like the spout of a teapot. Half an hour later, there it was at the water's edge, this time with the limb jutting out to the left, and at the base of it the cut-through creek emptying into the river. I had paddled something more than a mile to come something less than a hundred yards.

Profiting from this experience, I got sidetracked, if not lost for life, three times in the next two days, each time ending up in an "interior bayou" whose only exit was its entrance. There were morals here too—*the longest way round is the shortest way home* being the most obvious, but not necessarily the most important one. For one of these interior bayous, which I was to encounter the following day, just north of the state line, had a kind of ghastly beauty to it—its waters were motionless and covered with pollen, as though motes of sunlight had fallen there; its banks were no banks at all, but sinuous trees and shrubs—haws, birches, young cypress, and many I did not recognize—standing in the water, their reflections wavering and undulating in snaky vermiculations as the canoe slid by. I paddled up it to a dead end in one direction, and down it to a dead end in the other. It seemed an airless place, stygian even in the sunshine, worth visiting and worth leaving. I flushed the same deer three times trying to find a way out and never saw him, only heard his plunging panic. Bishop made much better time by stick-

ing to the main current, but I got more mileage.

But on the second day of the trip, with water slopping in the bottom of the canoe and the compass gyrating on the wanigan, I took no shortcuts, and got to the bridge at Freeland near midday. I pulled out on a sandbar, unloaded the canoe, and tipped the water out of it. At the edge of the woods there was a fine live oak, beneath which I could have my lunch and a nap, but first I scrambled up the embankment to the road and crossed the bridge. There was a filling station there—two gas pumps and a small cinderblock building, called Babson's, painted a pale green. I had told Daddy I would call from here, to make a progress report.

Inside were Kenneth and Anson Babson. Kenneth, a man in his fifties, ran the store; Anson was his father. He told me he was seventy-five years old and in poor health, pretty nearly living off his medicine now. But he was alert, and both father and son were forthcoming and helpful in a way that was beginning to seem specific to the upper Waccamaw. There was no pay phone, so Kenneth let me behind the counter to use the store phone. The local line was busy for a time, and then I got through and spoke briefly to Daddy. It seemed courtesy, after that, to buy something, so I picked out a couple of cream-filled, cellophane wrapped oatmeal cookies from the sparsely stocked shelf, and, as Kenneth

Babson was putting them into a small bag, his father chuckled, and said it was right poor picking today; a troop of Boy Scouts had come paddling down from Lake Waccamaw last week, stopped in, and just about cleaned the store out. Kenneth said it had been a bunch of them all right, and Mr. Babson nodded emphatically: "I looked out the window and it was a raft of them, just a reglar raft of them, out there in that river. I believe you could a' pulled 'em all abreast and walked straight acrost the river on them canoes."

I had no difficulty in turning our talk to other traffic on the river, and other days. I was interested in the log rafting. Lumber trucks and improved roads had put an end to it long before my time, and all I had for memory was a single raft, sunk in a lagoon not far from Conway, and visible in low water, when it provided a wonderful basking place for turtles. My father and his cousins in the lumber business remembered them well, and so, from a different perspective, did Mr. Babson. "What it was like was *work,*" he said. "Work. There weren't much way in this country to make money but lumber, and it's many the million board foot of pine and cypress gone right down this river, right by this place here." I asked how big a raft was, how many logs it had in it and how long the logs were. It was a question that betrayed my ignorance, and he was patient with me. "Now that would be a *clamp.* A clamp might have ten or twelve logs in it—be about fifteen foot across. Some'd be sixteen foot long, some twelve, depending on the quality of your logs. A raft was a whole bunch of clamps, one right after another. Be ten or twelve clamps to a raft. I believe more than that some time; some time I see 'em a quarter mile long, I do believe."

The clamps were pegged together. A sapling was laid across each end. He had seen his own father do it many and many a time. He would put the sapling right out at the end, so as to spoil as little lumber as possible. He used a one-inch augur with a long bit, and bored through the sapling and on down through the logs themselves. Then the pegs: "Weren't a question of goin' to the store and buying a dowel. What we had to have, we made. White oak trunnels was what my Daddy used. He'd cut him a good straight oak and split it out with a axe. Then he'd set down with a draw-knife and shape 'em. He made 'em square, one inch on the diagonal. He never measured nothing, but they'd be one inch on the diagonal, and the edges of them trunnels straight and sharp as mill-work. Many's the day I'd set and watch him make a blue hundred of 'em. When you pound oak trunnels down in that round hole, the edges bite right into the sides of the hole. And bein' in water, them trunnels swell up tight. You'd break the sapling before you'd pull 'em out."

The clamps were joined to each other by a sapling that operated like the coupling on a railroad car. This sapling was pegged to the center log of each clamp, and in this case the trunnel might be rounded off slightly, so that the sapling would pivot enough to permit a train—or raft—of clamps to negotiate a curve. At the same time, you would not want the sapling to pivot too readily, which would encourage the clamps to get out of line.

I was curious about the word he used for the oak pegs, and thought that perhaps "trunnel" was a corruption of "trestle" (always pronounced *trussel* around Conway) or "trundle" or "truss"; or that perhaps it was some merger of the three words, no one of which, as far as I knew, had any very logical connection to what he described. But it turns out that "trunnel" is simply "tree nail," its vowels having had their edges burred and rounded off by long, hard use. And that is what the work of logging and rafting was like: "My Daddy and them liked to fell the trees in the fall of the year, and leave 'em lie all winter. With cypress you didn't have no choice—a green cypress log'll sink like a lead pipe. Your pine would float green, but it'd float better dry, be lighter to handle. So you'd leave the whole tree to lie there, with the needles still on, to pull the sap out. Then haul 'em to the river in the spring time, when the freshet was on. You'd get 'em in the water and make up your clamps. The buyers would come up from Conway

(Mr. Babson gave it an extra syllable—Con-uh-way)—Burroughs or Stilley or Wilson—and they'd bid on the clamps. Once the price 'uz set, they'd put their mark on the logs and pay right there. That was tree-money. Then as I recall it, they'd pay so much a log to deliver; you'd get the delivery money at the mill. If you cut the tree yourself, and rafted it too, you'd be gettin' paid twice for the same log. But nobody ever done it would call it easy money." He looked at me with a certain air of happy discovery: "You work the log woods in them days, and you wouldn't think money growed on the trees around here. Trees was all the money they was, but it didn't no money grow on trees."

One clamp, somewhere toward the middle of the raft, was designated the kitchen. "If you had dry cypress logs, you'd use them for your kitchen—they'd float high. Have you a few planks there to make a surface, and you'd rig a tent. Cook-fire in a tin bucket or a lardstand. They'd take one big skillet and some meal and side meat or bacon, and that's about what they'd eat. Take seven days down to Conway." Even allowing for the freshet, it seemed incredible to me that something as unwieldy as a linked convoy of clamps—tons of dead weight, lying low in the water—could negotiate the perplexed convolutions of the Waccamaw: it would be like trying to get an intricately detailed, interconnected, and consequential set of proposals through a faculty meeting. They did not use ordinary poles, Mr. Babson said, but a pole with a two-pronged hook at the end. With this, they could push off from shore on the cove side, or snag a tree trunk, to warp around a point. "It would keep four or five men skipping," he said. "You had to be on the right clamp at the right time." As he remembered, the poles might be twenty feet long, and it wasn't always easy to disengage them from a tree you'd snagged. The raft, slow, but with an irreversible and mindless momentum, would keep going, and the rafter would wind up in the river.

"Course the river had a heap more water in it then. In my Daddy's time the steamboats used to come up from Conway, right up here to Freeland on the high water. Couldn't do that now. Waccamaw Lumber Company and St. Regis and G. P. must of spent a billion dollars altogether ditchin' and draining that swamp. What they done was taken water away from the Waccamaw and give it to the Cape Fear River. That's why the Waccamaw's got so much sand in it now. Back then, the freshets would flush it right out. And of course there weren't no trees laying in the water then; the rafters kept it cleant out. They had trouble enough without no trees." In spite of everything, rafts would pretty frequently get caught in the current and carried against the bank, or out into the swamp. They were too heavy for manpower to move, and so had to be broken up. Some logs might be saved, but many were lost. It was wet, wearing work, and when the logs were finally delivered to the mill in Conway, the rafters would set out on foot, a fifty-mile walk, back up to Freelands or Pireway. They would always know somebody's cousin or brother-in-law along the way, and take supper and spend the night there, and would arrive home late in the evening of the second day. "My Daddy would be used *up*. When he come back from Conway, it looked like that river washed all the starch right out of him. But he'd always have something for us—sweets or marbles or snuff."

Kenneth let his father do most of the talking. When he did speak he was stolid and careful, weighing the cost even of words: "It's better lumber layin' on the bottom of the Waccamaw River to this day than anybody'll ever see grow in Green Swamp again. Last summer them Gore boys pulled three thousand foot of clear cypress logs out, on the low water. Been settin' there sixty-seventy year." This led conversation around to Thomas Spivey and his uses of cypress. Both Babsons were pleased to have a chance to speak of him. "He's a *skilled* man," Kenneth said, "and you won't find a nicer fellow. Always glad to talk to you. He'll take you fishing or give you his bottom dollar. People say him and his Daddy live like Indians back in there, but he knows right where he is and he's where he wants to be. All that mess in New York and Washington, he don't worry about it none. And he's a better man for not worryin' about it." He shrugged. "Can't do nothin' about it no way. They got that mess up there and we're gettin' it down here, fast as we know how to."

He paused at this, puffed out his cheeks a little, and considered things, and his father took up the theme. He talked in the way that old men are privileged to talk, about the loss of coherence and proportion. There was too much money for too little work now, and pride had gone out of the work. Yet he was not one of those men who project upon the outer world the bitterness of their own loss of strength and consequence. His tone was bemused. In this quiet place on a country road, beside a river that you could wade across at low water, he had lived to see a lot, even though the scene surrounding him had not changed extremely or abruptly— mules had slowly given way to automobiles and tractors; the Waccamaw, diminished from the days when his father had rafted it, no longer sent its tribute of logs down to the mills in Conway. There had been men with crosscut saws; now there were the big new tree harvesters, with their mighty hydraulic shears: "It might be a actual woman settin' there in the cab of one of them things, working the levers and drinking herself a Pepsi." I asked Mr. Babson if he thought people were happier in his father's time.

Kenneth, who had been leaning on the counter and listening with a frown, spoke up: "People call it the good old days. But I tell you, it wurn't as good then as it is now." He looked at me. "You come in here to call you up your Daddy. All you got to do's pick up the telephone right behind this counter here and call. Now he ain't worried none; he ain't got to fret hisself half to death about where you are and when you gettin' home. He can just go right on about his business. Me or Daddy get a bad tooth, all we got to do is get in that truck out there and drive over to Whiteville and take it to the dentist and have him pull it right out, and we won't feel nothing. Used to be, you had a bad tooth, somebody'd take this here file," and he picked up an ordinary rat-tailed file from beneath the counter, "and just gouge it out." He illustrated, gouging the file-handle into the counter top, looking persuasively at us all the time, like a salesman demonstrating a product. "Just gouge it out with a file, like prizing out a stump with a pry-bar. Wurn't no dentist for you to go to. Wurn't no car and no good road to take you there. Wurn't nothing but a durn rat-tail file gougin' you in the jaw. Don't tell me about no good old days." He puffed out his cheeks again, and fell silent, as though abashed by the vehemence that had come over him when he picked up the file. It had to have been something that he had seen or heard of; you don't get that excited over a purely hypothetical instance of oral excavation.

Mr. Babson agreed that those days had been hard. We were having a discussion, not an argument, and he was scrupulous to do justice to the hardship. He still thought mostly of the log woods. "No chainsaws then. Just a crosscut and a axe. You might be working waist deep in water, with moccasins and mosquitoes all summer, and about freezing to death in winter. It was rough work, and it wurn't no workingman's compensation if you got hurt. A man cut off his finger, he'd just have to wrap a handkerchief round it and go right on, if he had any idea of feedin' his family that week. And buildin' tram roads was rougher. Eight-foot gum cross-ties, lay 'em right out in the swamp, and maybe get paid a dollar a day." But he went on, qualifying and gainsaying himself at times, hard to follow in his logic, but the images were clear enough. It seemed like he couldn't decide whether his thesis was to be that the good old days hadn't been altogether good, or the bad old days hadn't been altogether bad. An old man, not able to get around much now, he kept returning to the freedom of those days, when if you wanted you some wood for fuel or trunnels, you went out in the swamp and cut what you needed, and nobody to say you nay; and when you wanted some straw or moss or a mess of fish or ducks, you went and got that too. It was not there

58

for the asking, but for the taking. It was clear that people hadn't asked much in those days.

I finally left. They said to come back some day, maybe a little later in the year, when the river was right and the fishing was good. I said I would like that. Then I went back over to the sandbar, ate my lunch, and stretched out beneath the live oak. It was warm enough for me to take off my parka and roll it up for a pillow, but the sand was cool, as though still moist. The light glinted and danced through the dark canopy of the oak, and the river smell in the packed sand was fresh, the same smell that you get on your hands when you handle a live bream or redbreast from these waters. I drifted into the momentary sleep that lets things go fluid and immaterial in the mind; the inner language blurs and merges, resolves dissolve, and then something snubs you up short, and you are wide awake without having been fast asleep.

It was midafternoon when I got back into the canoe. I would paddle for two more hours, then pick the first good sandbar I came to. That would leave plenty of daylight to make camp and cook by. Mr. Anson Babson had grown up in a world paced by mule wagons, and the flow of the river, and a man walking. That now seemed to belong to a mythic dispensation, too archaic to possess even an archaeology—it survived only in the hesitant assertions of an old man's memory, and in turns of local speech. Once those things were gone, Freelands would be simply any other small speck on the map, a place where the action wasn't, and its past would amount to a cypress log, missed by the Gore boys on low water, buried on the river bottom.

I paddled without urgency, and felt my luck in having encountered the Spiveys and the Babsons. Their lives and stories carried in them the old lore of this river. In a colder mood, I would know that Thomas Spivey and Mr. Anson Babson were souvenirs of my trip, although I could not take them back to Conway and turn them over to the historical museum. But the pulse of the current and the steady work of the paddle, on a Monday afternoon in early spring, temporarily ratified an older chronology than the one that normally measured my life. There was no shortage of sandbars to choose from, and no one waiting and worrying. It had been another piece of luck to have seen in the cold rain of yesterday morning that people were still baptized in this river, came to it in a perfectly sombre mood to recreate themselves.

I found my sandbar in the shank of the afternoon, with the sun just above the treetops. Somebody had camped there before—there was a river birch with a few nails driven into it, perhaps to anchor a clothesline or a tent guy, and three willow prongs were stuck up in the sand, as rests for fishing poles. But everything was clean, and the sandbar, on the east bank, caught the last of the afternoon sun. A dead pine, its top broken off, stood at the edge of the woods, and I sawed it down, bucked it up, and split enough of it to provide kindling. It was as dry and sound as a telephone pole, and burned with an almost smokeless intensity. Looking at the river through the wavering heat above the fire was like looking through one old pane of wrinkled glass at another, which lay flat on the ground, reflecting the sky and the trees. There was no wind, and the light flakes of ash rose on the column of hot air and drifted away into some downy oblivion, idle and inconsequential as daydreams rising out of the day's business.

But I busied myself sufficiently, pitching the tent, then setting up a kitchen of sorts on the sandbar. It was cold enough to make movement welcome, and to make the cooking of supper as good as the eating of it. Supper was navy beans mixed with highly seasoned, home-cured sausage—as fine fuel, in its way, as the dead pine, and even finer when washed down with the chalky astringency of a splendidly cheap French wine of uncontrolled appellation. Then I squatted by the edge of the river to wash the supper dishes, scouring them with the coarse, clean sand and rinsing them in the current. The water was warmer than the air, and my wet hands tingled. The fire was almost noiseless behind me,

but the air was aromatic with pine. I rinsed my face in the river and then, ablutions completed, sat with my back propped against the plywood box. The river darkened to ink, and the single birch tree slowly became a silhouette and a sentinel against the evening light. A squirrel called from the swamps across the river, sounding a little querulous and unsure as owl-light closed down around him.

The canoe was safely tethered. I sat by the fire until the stars all were out, then covered the fire with sand, crawled into the tent and down into the sleeping bag. It felt silky and cold. I read a page or two and fell asleep. The night passed. I waked every hour, punctual as if there had been a watchman calling out the hours, and lay listening for a few minutes. There was no watchman, but there were barred owls, upriver and down, and not far away. They did more than hoot; they yelped, whined, and bayed with a kind of laughter, and then clucked and chuckled their way down through a sinister descrescendo. It was ululation enough of warlocks to curdle the dreams of fretful squirrels and blight their unborn babies. I cannot sleep if there is a clock ticking in the room or my neighbor's dog is barking, but this demonic cacophony would only interest me and lull me at the same time, and then I would come awake again, without realizing that I had ever gone back to sleep, and it would be an hour later. Once or twice during this night and the nights that followed there would be a heavy splash out in the river, or a vague rustling in the undergrowth, a suggestion that I was among mysteries continuous with those of sleep.

This night was cold, and coldest as the day came on. I went out into a white fog. Ice crystals lay in a lacy fringe at the downstream end of the sandbar, where there was a little backwater out of the current, and my wet socks and dishrag, which I had hung from a nail on the birch, had stiffened into mortal rigor. But the fire still smoldered beneath the sand, germinated quickly when I uncovered it, and soon was snapping briskly at some splinters of pitchy pine. By tradition I should have set bacon to sizzling in a blackened pan, but it was simpler to boil a few eggs in water, then use the water to make coffee, and drink it, and eat one of the eggs with a piece of somewhat resinous toast. The other eggs I kept for lunch, when they might be chased to admiration by a few swallows of the wine. In anticipation of that, I wrapped the bottle, frosty from its night on the bar, in a dishtowel, and stashed it deep in the plywood box, hoping to preserve some of its coolness until noon.

A one-night stand is just long enough to intimate all the things that time and familiarity would take away. I broke camp quickly, with the brusqueness of somebody sent to repossess the furniture from somebody else's house. A small willow, its leaves just unfurling, shivered faintly in a breeze I could not feel, and the bank of fog began breaking up into drifting scarves of mist, a troop of departing spirits. By the time I had gotten two corners below my campsite, the first shafts of sunlight were falling slantwise across the river, the last wisps of fog were giving up the ghost, and a demystified, lucid morning opened out ahead of me. Yesterday a red-shouldered hawk had called the day to order, and got its business underway. Today it was a pileated woodpecker: a staccato drum-burst against a hollow tree, then the bird itself. It flew across in front of me, with its peculiar alternation of flap, swoop, and collapse, and its last swoop fetched it up against the trunk of a cypress. It clung there a moment, cocked and primed, a perfectly congruous mixture of Woody Woodpecker, frocked-coated nineteenth-century deacon, and pterodactyl. Then it gave the tree an abrupt, jackhammer strafing, rolled out its lordly call, and swooped away, leaving the day to its own devices.

# 3 Pireway to Kingston Lake

The river remained preposterously sinuous. I was well below the vast floodplain of Green Swamp, where the high-water mark had never been more than six inches above the present level of the river. I could now see from the growth of moss and from faint, trim bands of pollen, which ran from tree trunk to tree trunk in strict parallels, straight and true as wire fencing or a surveyor's string, that here the river had at one point this spring been about forty inches above its present level. I tried to improvise an understanding of hydraulic logic to account for the consistent pattern of cove and point. On the cove, or outer, side of the bend, the land was higher—usually above the high-water mark. The point side was always below the high-water mark, and almost always ended in a sandbar. I supposed that this illustrated something like centrifugal force—the current on the outer edge of the curve moved faster, and cut deeper, eating away at the low banks of the floodplain until it brought the river to older, higher, and drier land, which was solid enough to deflect it. As the cove side lost ground, the point side gained it. Soil and sand from upstream precipitated out in the slower currents and eddies on the inside arc of the bend, slowly building up newer, and hence lower, land. Sand, the heaviest of the sediments, was the first to settle; it formed the newest land of all, still as clean and barren of vegetation as the river bottom itself.

Over the course of centuries and scores of centuries, the river would writhe slowly but continuously across the floodplain, making its way in moving coils and loops, smoothing and shifting sand and earth the way an eel would, if you put the eel on a beach, and let him squirm back to the sea. In a few places I could see current events as they shaped the course of fluvial history: there would be the familiar pattern of a long reach running east or west or even northward, then doubling a point and coming back in the opposite direction. But somewhere along the line, perhaps in a year of unusually high water, the river would have shown the vulnerability of an army with an overextended flank, or an argument grown so involved with developing and extending the logic of its own points that it loses the point it originally had sought to make. When this happened the river would break through and cut across the point, making a new channel, and turning the old one into an oxbow—a stagnant loop off the main flow of the river. As far as I could tell, the "interior bayous" of which Hall had spoken so direly to Bishop were parts of an earlier channel, which had dropped out of circulation. Sand levees had gradually built up and completed their isolation, except in times of high water.

But some of these interior bayous would be located within a point, indicating that they had been formed in the opposite way, and were direct routes that had been cut off and left behind when the river had meandered away from its apparent purpose. It was as though there were two impulses at work: one favored complication, circumlocution, and obliquity, and was always correcting and being corrected by the other, which appealed to common sense, and urged the straightforward, direct path from the source to the sea. Elaboration and simplification continually explained each other away, and neither held the advantage. I found that I could never anticipate where a lake or bayou might be, although when I encountered one, it was easy enough to rationalize how it came to be there. In my hands at least, fluvial geology was an improvised discipline, like history or psychology or economics— it could provide an explanation, or the appearance of an explanation, for why things were as things were, but it had no predictive value at all, and its chief function, perhaps, was to occupy the mind.

The Babsons had told me to be on the lookout for a fine old house at Reeves's Ferry, which was being restored by its present owner. They reckoned it was the oldest building in their section of the world, and when I came to it, before mid-morning, I thought them right, and got out for a closer look. There were signs of work in progress—rolls of tarpaper and insulation, bundles of clapboards and shingles—but no one was around. The house was a pleasant two-story building, with outside chimneys at each end and a single-storied ell extending out the back. It perched at the very brink of the river—with a running start, you could have dived into deep water from the front porch. It had no trace of antebellum swagger, none of that rhetoric of column or portico. Its best feature was a double breezeway—one, transecting the ell, divided what would have been the kitchen from the rest of the house. This was a familiar enough arrangement—you could find it in any number of tenant houses in the South, and it served to separate the heat and smell of cooking from the main body of the building. The other breezeway intersected this one the way the nave intersects the transept, and made in effect an open hallway through the main house. Standing at the intersection of the breezeways, I could look right through the house and out at the river. It was like looking through a covered bridge. In that slightly furtive mood that an empty house imposes on even an innocent trespasser, I walked through this central breezeway and out onto the front porch, which caught and kept the heat of the morning sun. I put my face to a parlor window and looked in, and saw a bare room, its walls and ceiling full of a wavy and rippling sunlight reflected up from the water.

Bishop mentions a store and a turpentine distillery at Reeves's Ferry, and it seemed likely that the building I was in had formerly combined a commercial and a domestic function. A gangplank could have easily been run out from the front porch to a raft or steamboat, and the breezeway would have allowed for the easy passage of goods and stock through the house. I wandered around outside, hoping some workmen might show up. There was a family burial plot just upstream from the house; most of the incumbents were named Smith, and the patriarch, judging from the relative size and antiquity of his stone, was Henry Cannon Smith, who was born in 1828 and died seventy years later, and who would have seen the price of turpentine fluctuate as dramatically and erratically as the level of the river itself: high in the 1840s and 1850s, plunging to almost nothing during the years of war and blockade, making a recovery, much abetted by the Franco-Prussian War, in the early 1870s, falling off badly again during the second half of that decade, then resurging tremendously in the early 1880s, and finally going into terminal decline at about the time he himself died.

Below the graveyard was a landing; the actual ferry and turpentine still had probably been located here. In this hinterland of backwoods and small farms, this must once have seemed a busy place. It would have been the sole nexus of economic exchange, where manufactured goods could be bought, where there would have been mules and wagons bringing barrels of scrapings to the distillery, log rafts being made up in the springtime, the ferry plying across the river, and the occasional excitement of a steamboat, huffing and puffing with all the self-importance of navigation, full of the news and rumors of wars and prices.

I walked up from the landing and graveyard to where the land opened out into fields, bordered by pines. The earth was freshly ploughed, a tractor stood at the far edge of the field, gleaming in the spring sun. But there was no farmer, as there had been no workmen, and I got back into my canoe very little the wiser about Reeves's Ferry.

By midday, I was at the Pireway Bridge, where we had seen the baptism, and here the river opened out into a blank, broad expanse of water, the first of Mr. Gore's "wretches." This stretch extended for about a mile and made for dull paddling, but then the river turned sharply to the east, resumed its deviousness, and regained its interest. Late in the afternoon I came upon a man in a big fiberglass bass boat, anchored and fishing with live bait and a cane pole around the top of a fallen tree. He told me that I was now in South Carolina—there had been a sign nailed to a cypress back upstream a ways, but it was easy to miss, he said, and he told me that just below I would find Wortham's Landing, and plenty of good dry ground for camping.

The landing was on the east bank. When Bishop had come down the river, there had been a bridge here, the only one between Lake Waccamaw and Conway. It had been built by the eponymous James Wortham, had disappeared sometime before the beginning of the twentieth century and been replaced by a ferry, which remained in operation until 1940. That a bridge existed at all at that early date and on this stretch of river invites some speculation—in a thinly settled county, with poor roads and with Conway the only community large enough even to be called a village, the river was in general a means of transportation, and not an obstacle to it. But Wortham must have had large holdings on the west side of the river, and, as Bishop points out, the Waccamaw at Wortham's Landing, or Wortham's Ferry, or Wortham's Bridge, lies only five miles west of Little River, which is the name of both a community and a short, but navigable, tidal river. It was never much of a port, but Wortham presumably saw an advantage in using it, instead of shipping everything downriver and out through Georgetown. Bishop himself, who identified with the confident and improving spirit of his age, imagined how easily a canal might be cut from the Waccamaw to the coast, establishing a direct link between this region's vast resources of timber and naval stores and the northern markets.

But nothing came of these schemes. On the corner above the landing that preserves Wortham's name, a wood-duck flushed ahead of me and flew squealing away, then flared, and a shot rang out. I drew abreast of the landing in time to see a man getting hurriedly into a pick-up truck. He gave me a look, gunned the truck, and departed, a guilty thing fearful of a summons. A little casual summer duck shooting on a spring afternoon was an old and established custom in Horry County, and I ought to have been happier than I was to see tradition perpetuated. I looked closely at the bank opposite the landing, but could find no sign of where any road had ever come down to the river. There was only the usual low swamp, the tangled oblivion of second-growth cypress and tupelo, pine and poplar, which had for so long sustained, withstood, and absorbed economic enterprises along the upper Waccamaw.

Wortham's Landing itself had a sleepy, under-utilized look; there was a newish brick house, of the style typical of a respectable Southern suburb, perched on a bluff overlooking the river and the landing. Below it, just downstream from the landing and right along the river, was a hog-lot; a stolid sow peered out from beneath her drooping ears. I continued on far enough downstream to escape the stink and scrutiny of pigdom, found a patch of dry woods on the west bank, and camped there. The spot was recommended only by a dilapidated beaver lodge that lay in a heap at the water's edge. After I had eaten, as the light faded, I sat on the bank above the lodge and eventually a single beaver swam up. Beaver had been extirpated from Horry sometime early in its history; my father had never seen or heard of them there, and their memory, like Mr. Wortham's, was preserved only in a few place names—Beaver Dam Swamp or Beaver Dam Creek. But then sometime in the

1970s they had begun filtering back, catching people by surprise, plugging culverts, flooding cornfields, and generally busying themselves with projects of reclamation and improvement. Their sign—peeled sticks and gnawed saplings—had become common along the river and throughout the county, but this was the first one I had actually seen. He represented one form of Northern industry and enterprise that I could regard with unmixed satisfaction, and I did so until he sensed my presence, and slipped quietly beneath the water.

The first owls had started by the time I went into the tent. I slept to their cacophony and got up, in the chill expectancy of dawn, before the last of them had ceased. I felt a focussed anticipation about the day ahead of me, which would take me through stretches of river that I knew from twenty-five or thirty years ago. I had hardly seen them since, but they were all part of the sharply specific memory of fishing: an overhanging oak, a cypress standing out in the current just downstream from a creek mouth, a row of young willows beside a shallow, sandy-bottomed run. These images were the most local of local knowledge, places where something had happened or something could be anticipated— where once a big, bad-tempered water-snake had dropped from the oak and landed, to his surprise and mine, in the boat, or where a good bass always lay, or where redbreast could be found in the fall. River-fishing, wherever it is done, is always the knowledge of such places, and the knowledge is particular, nontransferrable, and exact to the inch and the half inch, to the precise spot where the plug must be cast in against the buttressed stump of a cypress, back under overhanging branches. The paddler had to station the boat just so, and hold it back against the current; the fisherman had to be careful and unhesitating with the cast. When the cast was right there would be, it seemed, a hush of watching and being watched as the plug—a bright, buoyant, cocky-looking contrivance—sat there in a circle of spreading ripples and then sometimes, just often enough, a quiet, lazy swirl and the plug would disappear and the fish would be on.

Mostly, my knowledge of these places had come to me through Daddy, first his stories, then his pointing them out, and finally our fishing them together, and it seemed to me inalienable, as self-knowledge is said to be. I would know each place in relation to the landings—Bellamy's Landing, Star Bluff, Little Savannah, Red Bluff, Hardee's Ferry—where our expeditions began, but had only the haziest idea of the river distance between landings. It was like the way we remember episodes from early childhood— as clear, detailed images floating free of their spatial and temporal circumstances—and now I would renew these images with the whole river, from Lake Waccamaw down to Winyah Bay, as context. But I was without the rod or pole, and that tensing of attention that had brought the places into focus and clicked the shutter.

The weather was cool and bright again, but with a new softness and fragrance in the air, the first hints of sultriness to come. This would be my longest day of paddling, and I kept to the outside of the bends, letting the current do the work. The river, narrowing between sandy banks, picked up speed below Wortham's; every snag and stob looked like it was swimming earnestly upstream, pumping against the current and spreading a wake of silver bubbles out behind. I was on the water before sunrise, and so could watch the woods, and the river that reflected them, grow chromatic—the soft blended greens of early spring, and the pastel blush, somewhere between peach and apricot, of the water oaks and laurel oaks.

This had been the country of the turpentiner, the tar-heel. Other vocations of the American frontier—the cowboy, the lumberjack, the prospector, the trapper—went on to assume a heroic dimension, and to elevate their landscapes into icons of national significance. But the turpentine woods had no romance of mobility and open spaces, no theme of conquest or discovery. There was first the destitution and transience of the frontier without its adventure of hope, and then a landscape left unenhanced by memory or regret. You could still find the occasional scarred tree, or a shallow depression in sandy soil, marking the site of an old tar kiln. For Gilmore and Bishop, the gloomy swamps and woods of the upper Waccamaw had had an exact corollary in the illiterate, rudimentary human culture they found in this region, and they saw it as most men of their century would have seen it—purely in terms of its backwardness, its opportunities for investment and capacity for progress. Now, more than a century later, the citizens were literate and acculturated, but the landscape was not. The oaks that glowed softly in the early sunshine made no allusions and responded to none. Their beauty seemed mute, indifferent, and unclaimed.

I was in earshot of Bellamy's Landing, where S.C. Route 9 crosses the river, for nearly an hour before I got there. First I heard what sounded like a man hammering on a tin roof, quite near at hand. With the twisting of the river, the sound came first from one bank and then from the other, and, as I drew closer, its quality changed, becoming more massive and regular. To this were gradually added other sounds of heavy machinery, creaking, thumping, and scraping, and I could eventually see a low cloud of white dust rising over the swamp.

This seemed ominous, and the first confirmation of the omen came just above the bridge. I rounded a bend and found on the east bank what was no longer swamp or piney upland, and was not yet a vacation community or golf course, but was simply Investment. An area of perhaps a hundred acres had been stripped and bulldozed; except for a few oaks that had been spared and some mounded heaps of slash and underbrush, the place was as barren as a beach. A road came in on the far side of the clearing, and there were four enormous piles of earth there. A red-shouldered hawk flapped heavily across the clearing, landed in one of the surviving oaks, teetered awkwardly there for a moment, and took flight again, passing directly over me and disappearing upriver.

I had no idea who or what was behind this particular enterprise, but its outlines were familiar. On the upper Waccamaw in 1874,

Bishop could not believe that the prevailing destitution and backwardness were unalterable; they were simply the consequence of slavery, war, and the corruptions and ineptitudes of Reconstruction. He addresses his Northern readers:

> The railroad has become one of the great mediums of enlightenment to mankind, and joins in a social fraternity the disunited elements of the country. God grant that the resources of the great South may soon be developed by the capital and free labor of the North. Our sister states of the South, exhausted by the struggles of the late war which resulted in consolidating more firmly than ever the great Union, are now ready to receive every honest effort to develop their wealth or cultivate their territory. Let every national patriot give up narrowness of views and become acquainted with (not the politicians) the people of the New South, and a harmony of feeling will soon possess the hearts of all true lovers of a government of the people.

National patriotism wasn't necessarily the motive, or harmony of feeling the consequence, but the movement of Northern capital into this region had indeed taken place, and had made its economic growth possible. Prosperity had come; a few miles east of where I sat lay land that in my youth had supported only scrub oak, stunted pines, sea oats, and myrtle thickets, and that in my father's youth had been the sort of property that was generally willed to daughters, because it was worthless for farming. It now commanded tens of thousands of dollars per acre, and had sprouted condominiums, golf courses, and residential enclaves, the most exclusive of which had gates with guards on duty twenty-four hours a day, making certain that poverty and ignorance never returned to that vicinity.

Along the coast now, Myrtle Beach and North Myrtle Beach had run out of waterfront, and were even running out of what might be called scenery. The beaches were eroded and the dunes were gone. The salt marshes, swashes, and small tidal inlets—heron-stalked, raccoon-haunted places that in my youth teemed with mullet and shrimp, crab, pinfish, and flounder, and echoed to the cry of willets and terns—had been dredged, filled, or dammed; two or three of them, scarcely more than ditches, were still visible, but most had only a nominal existence. Recreational investment had to turn elsewhere, and the Waccamaw was the logical place.

There is no special classification or organized sentiment to protect the Waccamaw. It isn't wild or scenic in ways that we have learned to recognize. People have always lived along it, here and there, wherever high land came down to water, and they have done with their land very much as they wished. The river was taken for granted, a mundane fact with a long, unpunctuated, unheeded history of casual use and abuse. Its swamps had been cut and re-cut, logs had floated down it; steamboats had churned up it; much of its watershed and many of its tributaries had been drained. It was a convenient place to dump the largely organic refuse that even the poorest farms generate, and I have on occasion seen dead dogs in it, or cats, a pig or two, and once even a mule.

That the river remained largely clean was a reflection of the relative backwardness and simplicity of the county and the lives through which it flowed. People's attitude toward it resembled their attitudes toward their own history—it was constant and unremarkable, too familiar to be clearly seen or understood or compared to anything else. It was there to fish in—the number of hours spent by men and boys in small boats, and by whole families squatting on the bank, cane poles in hand, would defy calculation—but the fishing was not spectacular. It was merely fishing, an ordinary amenity of rural and small-town life, and not a thing to make a big commotion about, or to notice until it was gone. Nobody was going to flag down a caterpillar tractor with half a dozen hand-sized bream and redbreast threaded onto huckleberry stem.

The scalped and graded acres in front of me implied the bleakest view of historical inevitability. Investment had come here because the Waccamaw was comparatively unspoiled, and investment would predictably oppose any effort to keep it that way. In this booming and disappearing county, every infringement upon a natural system—river, marsh, or beach—became a justification for further infringement, until the argument that there was no longer anything worth saving had fulfilled itself. I didn't go ashore, but let the current take me around the corner and into sight of Bellamy's Landing. Bridgework was in progress—a new span was being added, to accommodate two more lanes of traffic. A big crane was driving pilings—that was what I had been hearing—and there was a hubbub of earth-movers, caterpillars, and jackhammers, punctuated by the staccato of pneumatic drills, the shrilling of electrical saws, and, as a sort of comic *leitmotif*, the diminutive, two-toned beeping of heavy machinery being driven in reverse.

There had always been a store at Bellamy's Landing, and so I stopped, wanting to replenish my water jug and stretch my legs. The woman at the cash register could tell me nothing about what was going on upstream—"it's *somebody's* business, honey, but it sho' ain't mine. All that work they doin' on the highway, 'bout the only thing comes in my door these days is *dust*"—and she sold me a six-pack of beer and told me I could get water from a tap out back. I thanked her, filled my jug, and returned to the canoe. When I paddled under the bridge, the air around me vibrated with noise, the way it does when a train pulls into an underground station.

I concentrated on putting physical and psychological distance between myself and Bellamy's Landing. The river was discolored for some distance below the construction site, but within a mile it was flowing as black and bright as it had been at its beginning, and I was stopping again, this time to look up at an osprey nest in the top of a dead cypress. The birds looked back, and didn't like what they saw. The female sat tight on the nest, her head aimed down at me, her eye an unblinking glare. She lifted her crest, and it gave her that look of spiky, wild dishevelment that makes an osprey resemble a prophet newly arrived from the wilderness, brimming with apocalyptic disclosures and truths that burn in the utterance. But she had no capacity for utterance beyond a rising string of plaintive, high-pitched, monosyllabic yips, after which she paused, her beak still open, as though parched and maddened by her failure. The male circled above the nest, also yipping.

When you travel by river, you discover something about roads. When you drive, the road defines the landscape, which becomes only the soiled and slovenly corridor through which you move, a measurement of the time you have passed and the time that lies ahead of you. But rivers both define and express a landscape, and they do it slowly, organically, and profoundly, the way a history defines and expresses a culture. From the water, roads seem adventitious and inconsequential; the occasional bridge no more disturbs the river than the vapor trail of a passing jet disturbs the vastness of the sky. Here with the ospreys, the Waccamaw seemed untouched and untouchable, and it was a great temptation to forget that it was neither.

By noon, I had reached Star Bluff, the most appealingly and mysteriously named of all the upriver landings. The day was making good its promise of warmth, and, although the sun was shining and the dome of the sky was a soft blue, there was a whitish cast to the horizon, and I could feel the silent recruiting and mustering of rain. I bent my back, to get as far downriver as I could before it came. The river continued sandy-bottomed and serpentine—Star Bluff had been famous redbreast water—but the middle of the day is not the time to see a place. The natural world goes comatose, ceases to stir, sing, or feed; the sense of freshness and possibility fades. There was a house at Star Bluff that had not been there in my boyhood, and yet it did not look new. A dog lay in the front yard, and when he saw the canoe, he roused himself up and came down to the edge of the water, where he stood and barked and wagged his tail, half watchdog and half welcoming committee. But I plugged away at the paddle—stroke, twist, pry, return, over and over, pushing through the doldrums, the tediums, the blank continuums that merely serve to hold space and time together.

I had fished upriver and down from Star Bluff, but not very frequently, and I could not tell whether it was that today I had passed so quickly out of familiar territory, or whether the familiar territory had passed so largely out of my memory. I kept looking, in the bright lifelessness of noon, for places I would recognize, but below Star Bluff the river had only a generic look of familiarity, as though it expected me to recognize it, but was too proud to give me a hint. And then, much quicker than seemed right or possible, I came to a cut-through where every detail was in place: the sandbar at the head of the cut and the pocket of black water between the lower end of the sandbar and the bank; the oaks and maples that arched over the channel; the stobs and snags at the foot of the cut, where it rejoined the river.

This was the Montgomery Landing cut-off, and it did not belong to the Star Bluff territory at all. It marked the upper limit of the water we fished from Little Savannah. In those days, it had seemed a long way above Little Savannah, but then in those days I had thought of Star Bluff as being on a part of the river that had only the most distant and attenuated affiliation with Little Savannah, where, when I was twelve or fourteen years old, Daddy and his friend, Mr. C. C. Harper (who was also my godfather) had built a cabin.

It would be more exact to say that they had assembled the cabin at Little Savannah. They had built it in sections—floor, walls, and roof—in our backyard in Conway, and then carried them up to Little Savannah by pick-up truck. The road in was muddy, rough, and treacherous, and each trip had an air of desperate adventure. When assembled ("C. C., you *sure* that ain't the floor we got on the roof?" "Hell no, man. That's the floor we just got through hanging the door in."), it was a single-roomed, shed-roofed, nine-by-twelve structure that looked like the overgrown and ungainly offspring of the outhouse that was located a few yards behind it. After a year or two, we added an eight-by-twelve screen porch. Nothing inside the cabin or out was ever painted, and its newness faded almost overnight into a weathered shabbiness; sitting a little unevenly on cement blocks, it looked purely natural and accidental, as though it had drifted down on high water, and been left stranded by the receding freshet. This illusion was furthered by the fact that the river would get to it almost every spring, cleansing it of its terrestrial grime and leaving instead a fine dusty coating of pollen and sediment, precisely corresponding to the high-water mark on the surrounding trees. "Good thing we didn't build it any tighter," Mr. Harper would say; "Might've floated away."

In a straight stretch which I knew to be just above the cabin, I met a fisherman paddling laboriously upstream in a flat-bottomed boat. He was setting trotlines for catfish, his baited lines laid out neatly on top of the fishbox. He more or less hailed me, as though there were some emergency, and asked if I had anything to drink. In Horry County, this is not always a simple question, so I answered circumspectly, and told him I had some water, but it wasn't cold. He spat emphatically over the side: "Nooo. I got *war-der*. I mean have you got anything *cole* to drink?" I said that I did happen to have a beer on board. He brightened up: "You ain't got two, is you? I'll buy 'em offen you." I gave him two beers and we chatted a little longer. He said the fishing hadn't been much, but it ought to start picking up now with the weather getting warm and the river dropping. I questioned him about distances, and he was vague—he wasn't sure whether I could get to Red Bluff by night-fall or not. Like most of the other people I talked to on the trip, he knew his own stretch of water, and had only a hazy idea of what lay more than a mile or two upstream or downstream of his particular landing. As it turned out, I reached Red Bluff in midaf-ternoon, almost before I was ready to.

I said goodbye to the trotliner, and rounded the corner above the cabin. In the first spring after the cabin was built, when the river was very high and the road into it was impassable, Daddy decided we should go up and check it out one Sunday, to see how it had survived the freshet. We had put in at Red Bluff and motored up, the river so high that we were continually running into our own wake, which travelled directly across the flooded points, while we had to circumnavigate them. In front of the cabin, a young sweetgum grew out horizontally from the bank, its roots half undermined by the river, and on this morning, as we approached, an otter, the first I had ever seen, sat there sunning. It saw us the instant we saw it, plunged into the river and disappeared, but that momentary vision of dark fur gleaming in the spring sunlight had seemed to me a portent of endless promise, confirming that our cabin was sited in a primeval place, where the wildest of creatures basked familiarly on its doorstep. But we never saw another otter there, or anywhere else on the upper Waccamaw, and the one we had seen came to seem like a last glimpse of a wildness our cabin had displaced, and not of a wildness that would receive us.

The horizontal sweetgum was, incredibly, still there, and looked no bigger than it had thirty years before, its growth perhaps exactly offsetting the general sense of shrinkage that you discover when you return to any childhood scene. And even more incredibly, I caught a quick, serpentine movement in the water, and there, as though by prearrangement, was an otter. It swam across the river ahead of me, directly in front of the cabin, its eye never leaving the canoe. When it reached the far bank of the river, it lay on the surface of the water, in the green reflection of a willow, and held its position against the current with a slow, sinuous sculling of the tail. The animal looked like a consolidation of the current itself, with the same wavering liquidity of a motion that neither advances nor retreats. The sun gleamed on its sleek head, which was turned toward me, watching me with the blank, unalarmed curiosity of a cat. I reached slowly for my camera, and when I did the otter changed, let its body sink down deeper into the water, and, with the click of the shutter, it disappeared without a ripple.

The cabin was still there. I could imagine Mr. Harper saying, from beyond his grave, that it didn't look any worse than the day it was built, which was pretty damn sorry. Daddy was the only one who used it now, coming out every spring to cut back the bushes, and putting a new roof on it every decade or so. These were acts of commemoration and devotion—it had probably been a quarter of a century since he had spent a night here. He could not even use it as a place to store tackle; the surest way to get it broken into was to leave something in it worth stealing.

The porch was, as always, unlocked—a lock would have only caused unnecessary tear, if not wear, on the screen panels—and it appeared that local fishermen had used it this spring, to take refuge from the rain or early mosquitoes. I didn't have a key to the cabin proper, and had no particular desire to go in. It had always been what a vacation home perhaps ought to be—a place that encouraged you to spend most of your time outside. With the early afternoon beginning to mass the weight of its heat and humidity, and the air thickening toward the somnolence of summer, even though spring had barely begun, I had a kind of palpable and external recollection, as though it were the day, the splintered boards of the cabin, the privy with its door, half unhinged, hanging ajar, the pump-stand in the yard, and the dry and dusty, faintly aromatic leaves of laurel oak underfoot that were doing the recollecting, and not myself. It seemed strange to hear only the raspy squeaking song of myrtle warblers, thin and early-vernal as the running of melt-water, and not the drowsy, buzzy hum of cicadas. My wife's grandmother was fond of saying, on the most beautiful afternoon of the summer, as the light glinted off Lake Sunapee and she drew a shawl around her shoulders, that in New Hampshire, you could always feel winter at your back. In South Carolina, then, you can always feel summer just beneath the skin. A good many mosquitoes hovered around my face, without actually biting, and it all strongly evoked the weekends we would spend here in late April or early May, when the fishing was at its best.

Once, in April, Mr. Harper had brought along a turkey call that somebody had given him. He showed it to us as we drove up. It might as well have been a unicorn call for all any of us knew about how to use it and for all the amusement, tinged with just the slightest, finest edge of credulity, with which we regarded it. There were five of us, Ricky McIver and I, and Mr. McIver, in addition to Daddy and Mr. Harper and Mr. Harper's melancholy and brainless pointer, Tip. That night, after supper and with the whiskey not yet put away, somebody got out the call and tried to make a noise with it, and then everybody tried, and then Mr. Harper put glasses on his big face and unfolded the instructions and solemnly read them to us. Then he picked up the call and scraped it as per the instructions. It sounded like chalk scraped across a blackboard; to improve the effect he held it under his chin like a violin and scraped some more. Tip broke into lugubrious moaning and went off into the darkness. Everybody laughed and we all went to bed.

Next morning, after fishing and breakfast and washing up, Mr. Harper sat himself down on the stoop of the cabin and pulled out the call. Tip slunk away under the truck at the sight of it. Mr. Harper held up his hand, magisterial as a quarterback silencing the crowd: "Now listen. How'm I going to seduce the wily gobbler with all you jokers carryin' on around here?" So everybody got sober and still and he scraped away a few times and then stopped. Then we all held our hands to our ears, in a pantomime of listening. It would have made a strange sight if somebody had happened to walk in upon it at that moment. But what happened instead was that there came, from far upriver, very rapid and faint as the sound of the sea in a seashell, a burst of gobbling. We got silent in earnest then, and Mr. Harper, in addition, got his shotgun out of the truck.

What I remembered now was the heat and silence of that morning, the strangeness of thinking about hunting in such weather, and my own conviction that, if the gobbler would just show himself, even let us see the sunlight spangling from the bronzed iridescence of his neck, it would be a sign, and I would know who and what I was, and have an important story to tell every single person I ever met. We all went down to the bank of the river, almost tiptoeing, and sat there with our feet dangling over the edge, and Mr. Harper scraped some more.

The gobbler answered twice, no closer than he had been the first time. Then there was a long interval, while Mr. Harper scraped and no answer came and we all began to get restless and skeptical. "Somebody's barnyard turkey cooped up in a pen," Mr. McIver said, and even though there were no farms close enough, that began to sound reasonable. There wasn't so much as the rumor of a wild turkey in this section of the county. But Mr. Harper kept it up, with a good deal of scoffing for accompaniment—"You ain't too *fetching* on that thing, C. C."—and he laughed and looked out from beneath his eyebrows with exaggerated sagacity and explained how, even as we spoke, the turkey was sneaking toward us, and we'd see him come busting into the clearing any minute, all hot and horny. And there was more joking about the shock the gobbler was in for when he found, instead of some delectable young hen, all two hundred pounds of Mr. Harper: "Collins Crawford, you want even *need* to shoot him." He stood up and tucked the call under his chin and dragged the scraper across the metal reed with excruciating deliberation. Tip moaned from under the truck and then, directly across the river from us, there was an abrupt, explosive gobble and the pummeling of heavy wings.

That was as close as the cabin ever came to filling the promise of the otter at its doorstep. We never saw the turkey. He answered the call once more, from far downstream, sounding not only faint and distant, but a bit indignant. I'm still waiting to see properly a wild turkey—not a half-domesticated one in a zoo, or a feral one in a game preserve, or even (as I once did manage to see) an unfettered one legging it hot-foot and roadrunner fashion across a county road. I am waiting to see one in an Horry County swamp, on his own ground about the wildest and most mythological thing that might still survive there. Compared to that, an otter or a fox or even a bobcat would be blatant and banal as a yard-dog.

It would have been nice, for old times' sake, to have camped at Little Savannah. But it was still early afternoon, with a great deal of daylight left to fill, and little way to fill it but by paddling. In the moist air of springtime—a pair of wet socks I had hung over the thwarts when I set out at daybreak were still damp, despite the bright sun—the line between comfortable and uncomfortable heat is thin, a matter of a few degrees. The day now approached that line. A few big gars rolled lazily in the middle of a wide bend just below the cabin. One stuck his needle nose out of the water with a respiratory wheeze, and I could see the strange golden disc of his eye. A spotted sandpiper bobbed and teetered along the edge of a sandbar, a dumbshow of anxiety and indecision, and finally took his stiff-winged flight low over the water, and landed a hundred yards downstream, still full of fidgets and second thoughts. Because I was looking at him as he genuflected and stuttered along the water's edge, I noticed an odd imprint in the sand, and paddled over and got out to look more closely.

It had been an alligator, and he had been lying with his body half out of the water. His paw prints were almost exactly the size of my hand; the impression left by the transverse scales of his belly looked a good deal like the track of a caterpillar or a snowmobile. I was surprised to see that one had been out this early, even before the snakes and turtles, and surprised again, two or three miles further downstream, when I flushed one from a steep bank. He appeared to be about my own size, and, legal protection and endangered species status notwithstanding, he went off the bank like a shot. In suburban ponds and (from what Bartram and other early travellers tell us) in wilderness conditions, alligators are indolent and insolent, surly, sluggish, and given to a sort of belligerent malingering, if not actual aggression. But they had been hunted for their hides and simply shot on the Mount Everest principle for long enough along the Waccamaw to have become shy as deer, and most of the ones I had ever seen had been glimpsed as this one was—a plunging motion like a sudden jet of dark water from a discharge pipe, gone before the eye could give it shape, and leaving only a short trail of bubbles on the surface to persuade you that you had seen anything at all.

Rowing his light canoe once he got below Old Dock, riding the high water, and not delayed or bemused by any association with the country he traversed, Bishop was almost a full day ahead of me by this point on the river. He had spent his second night at Pireway, and the third night had closed down around him somewhere near where I now was. With the river in flood, the water had been far out in the swamps. He had no map, to show him where dry land might be. It's his story:

Darkness settled on the swamps, and a heavy mist rose from the waters and enveloped the forest in its folds. With not a trace of land above water I groped about, running into what appeared to be openings in the submerged land, only to find my canoe tangled in thickets. It was useless to go further, and I prepared to ascend to the forks of a giant tree, with a light rope, to be used for lashing my body into a safe position, when a long, low cry engaged my attention.

"Waugh! ho! ho! peig—peig—pe-ig—pe-ig," came through the still, thick air. It was not an owl, nor a catamount that cried thus; nor was it the bark of a fox. It was the voice of a Cracker calling in his hogs from the forest. This sound was indeed pleasant to my ears, for I knew the upland was near, and that a warm fire awaited my benumbed limbs in the cabin of this unknown man. Pushing the canoe towards the sound, and feeling the submerged border of the swamp with my paddle, I struck the upland where it touched the water, and disembarking, felt my way along a well-trodden path to a little clearing. Here a drove of hogs were crowding around their owner, who was scattering kernels of corn about him as he vociferated, "pe-ig—pe-ig—pig—pig—pig." We stood face to face, yet neither could see the face of the other in the darkness. I told my tale, and asked where I could find a sheltered spot to camp.

The man's name was Wilson Edge, and, as Bishop seems to have anticipated, he insisted on sharing his own house and hearth. The house turned out to be a single-roomed log cabin, chinked with moss. Its roof was cypress shakes; the chimney was made of logs plastered with mud. But there was a big fire on the hearth sending out a blaze of light, and the cabin was tidy.

"Hog and hominy's our food here in the piny woods," said Mr. Edge, as his wife invited us to the little table; "and we've a few eggs now and then to eat with sweet potatoes, but it's up-hill work to keep the niggers from killing every fowl and animal we have. The carpet-bag politicians promised them every one, for his vote, forty

85

acres of land and a mule. They sed as how the northern government was a-going to give it to um, but the poor devils never got any thanks even for their votes. They had been stuffed with all sorts of notions by the carpet-baggers, and I don't blame um for putting on airs and trying to rule us. It's human natur, that's all. We don't blame the niggers half so much as those who puts it in their heads to do so; but it's hard times we've had, we poor woods folks. They took our children for the cussed war, to fight fur niggers and rich people as owned um.

"We never could find out what all the fuss was about; but when Jeff Davis made a law to exempt every man from the army who owned fifteen niggers, then our blood riz right up, and we sez to our neighbors, 'This ere thing's a-getting to be a rich man's quarrel and a poor man's fight.' After all they dragged off my boy to Chambersburg, Pennsylvania, and killed him a fighting for what? Why, for rich nigger owners. Our young men hid in the swamps, but they were hunted up and forced into the army. Niggers has been our ruin. Ef a white man takes a case before a nigger justice, he gives the nigger everything, and the white man has to stand [to] one side. Now, would you folks up north like to have a nigger justice who can't read nor count ten figgurs?"

I tried to comfort the poor man, by assuring him that outside of the political enemies of our peace, the masses in the north were honestly inclined towards the south now that slavery was at an end; and that wrong could not long prevail, with the cheerful prospect of a new administration, and the removal of all unconstitutional forces that preyed upon the south.

The two beds in the single room of the cabin were occupied by the family; while I slept upon the floor by the fire, with my blankets for a couch and a roll of homespun for a pillow, which the women called "*heading.*" They often said, "Let me give you some heading for your bed." We waited until eight o'clock the next day for the mists to rise from the swamps. My daily trouble was now upon me. How could I remunerate a southerner for his cost of keeping me, when not, in the true sense of the word, an invited guest to his hospitality?

Wilson Edge sat by the fire, while his wife and little ones were preparing to accompany me to see the paper boat. "Mr. Edge," I stammered, "you have treated me with great kindness, your wife has been put to some inconvenience, as I came in so unexpected a manner, and you will really oblige me if you will accept a little money for all this; though money cannot pay for your hospitality. Grant my wish, and you will send me away with a light heart." The poor Cracker lowered his head and slowly ran his fingers through his coal black hair. For a moment he seemed studying a reply, and then he spoke as though HE represented the whole generous heart of the south.

*"Stranger,"* he slowly articulated, *"Stranger, I have known white men to be niggers enough to take a stranger's money for lodgings and vittles, but I am not that man."* (Italics Bishop's)

Edges had still lived in this section when I was growing up; one of them ran a country store and an oyster roast out on Highway 905, half a mile from Red Bluff. Of Mr. Wilson Edge, it is recorded only that, at the end of May in 1863, a little more than a month before his son was to die in the Gettysburg campaign, he bought a tract of 300 acres, for 450 presumably Confederate and therefore severely depreciated dollars, "above Red Bluff, and binding on Council Bluff." Free-range hogs still roamed the swamps of the upper Waccamaw in the late 1950s, and farmers still called them, although it was difficult to imagine those slab-sided, rangy, and astonishingly quick animals complying as trustingly as Edge's did. Bishop's description of the call is extremely accurate—one could only add that the pitch rises sharply on the second syllable of *pe-ig*. But I wondered how far Bishop had done with Mr. Edge what any writer is tempted to do with a provincial and unsophisticated character—how far he had made Edge the spokesman for his own conception of simple verities and unadorned humanity. But even if Edge was to some extent a sentimentalization and an idealization, I was glad to have this record of one man's existence from a period of the county's history that must have been so full of tur-

87

bulence and trouble, and that remains so largely obscured. Bishop represents Edge's racism as being of a relatively paternalistic sort; and he indicates that his host's resentment was directed at least as much at slaveholders as it was at blacks and carpetbaggers. If I could judge from the impressions of my childhood, both of those things would change: the racism would lose any vestige of sympathetic understanding ("It's human natur, that's all"), and the very different perspectives and experiences of the planter and the subsistence farmer would be glossed over. The myth of the Lost Cause conveniently forgot how many white Southerners, like Mr. Edge, did their losing in a cause that, if it had prevailed, would have gained them nothing.

There is a bridge at Red Bluff and a good landing just downstream from it. Lines of ecological demarcation, like the lines that divide historical or geological epochs, are inexact and indistinct, and this is especially so on a river like the Waccamaw, which meanders uneventfully through a low, flat, formless terrain. The bridge and landing at Red Bluff look a great deal like the bridge and landing at Pireway. But, despite this, Red Bluff is about the point at which the upper Waccamaw becomes the middle Waccamaw. It grows less serpentine, slower and wider. On low water, the tide can make itself felt, as a complete slackening of the current, at Red Bluff. From here on down to Conway there are progressively fewer sandbars, and those few are not so white and inviting as the ones upstream. They are, in the strict sense of the word, *soiled* by the lighter sediments and silts that begin to precipitate out as the current loses speed. As you get further downstream from Red Bluff, you sense that the river is gaining a kind of maturity—deeper, more persistent in its course, more deliberate, better suited for the regularities of commerce. At the time of Bishop's trip, there would have been no appreciable river traffic, but within a decade, sidewheelers would be docking regularly at Red Bluff, picking up barrels of tar, pitch, and turpentine, bales of cotton, hogsheads of tobacco. The steamboats went further upstream, even as far up as Freelands, Mr. Babson had said; but that traffic would have been less frequent, more dependent upon the stage of the river.

To Mr. Edge, those first steamboats that came thrashing upriver must have looked like an arriving future; now they seemed the technological equivalent of dinosaurs—huge, unwieldy breathers of smoke and fire, in some elemental way they seemed older than canoes or log-boats, because they vanished so completely. In a few more weeks now, the landing at Red Bluff would be crowded with trailers and big bass boats and high-powered runabouts, and water-skiers would have the river sloshing within its banks like coffee in a cup. But for the present, it was preternaturally quiet. The sky turned solid gray by midafternoon; the long, flat stretches of water seemed sullen and monotonic in this light, as though it were a river of oil or grease. The thermometer was slowly falling, and with the air so laden with moisture, it seemed that you might sweat with the least exertion and then shiver as soon as you stopped.

A few miles downstream from Red Bluff, near what an old map calls the Todd's Ferry Landing, a party of four black women fished from the shore. Coming down close along the bank, I heard them first, then saw their long cane poles hanging out over the water, the tips of the poles not quite meeting their own reflections, pole and reflection sutured by the fishing line. Because I was hugging the bank and they were talking and tending their lines, the women did not see me until I was directly in front of them and only a few feet away. They stopped their conversation abruptly, and looked blank, as though a teacher or a spy had just entered the room. There is something uncivil about gliding unseen into what other people had assumed to be their privacy, and materializing suddenly before them. If they are black, and you are white, even at this late date of the Christian era, 111 years after Bishop had so earnestly hoped that true harmony of feeling might arise among the citizens of Horry, the incivility is compounded. If I had had

the wit to cough or clear my throat before I came upon them, I might not now have found myself the object of so stony a regard.

I asked how the fishing was, and for an uncomfortable time nobody answered, but finally the woman nearest me, never lifting her eyes from the tip of her pole, said "Nuttin," in an accent that made it clear that she'd rather have said nothing. Wondering if this were Todd's Ferry, I asked if this place had a name.

"Waccamaw River, far as ever I heared."

How far was it by river to Conway?

"Consid'able."

How far to Grahamville?

"Never heard of it."

I was not going to be able to make amends for my intrusion, so I wished her luck with the fishing, let go the cypress branch I had been holding, and picked up the paddle. The woman looked up now—the others remained studiously oblivious to us both—and relented slightly.

"You paddle that thing to Conuhway, you fixin' to be wet before you git there."

"You think it'll rain?"

"What I *think* don't matter. *Radio* say hit gwine rain this evenin.' Rain hard. Tomorrow too. Dat's what hit say." She turned and spat a jet of brown juice as vehement and precise as water from a water pistol. "What I think don't signify, rain er shine. No hit don't. You fixin' to be wet, thinkin' or no thinkin'."

I paddled away, expecting to hear their voices resume behind me, but they did not speak to each other for as long as I was in earshot.

I kept at it until six, when I reached the bridge below Bear Bluff. A wind, a surprisingly warm and steamy north-easter, had come up in midafternoon and helped push me along, and now the young maple and willow leaves were showing their silvery undersides. There was a good bank just below the bridge, and I pulled out there, taking the precaution of bringing up everything in the canoe and then the canoe itself, which I overturned and lashed down. I cooked and ate, then packed the cooking gear back into its boxes and stashed them under the canoe, sure of rain before morning. It would be best to have a cold boiled egg, a bit of cheese, and some juice for breakfast, and not to try to cook in the rain.

Then there was time to sit looking out over the river—broader here, and, despite the proximity of the road, lonelier feeling than it had been upstream. The wind was seething in the pines that sheltered me. Just at dark, two wood-duck flew from somewhere downstream, crying as they came, and, cupping their wings, pitched down on the opposite side of the river. I lost them when they dropped below the treeline, but saw the slashing hiss of silver wake they made when they hit the water. They called once more in the only voice they have, which always sounds full of distress and urgency, even when they are in the safety of a darkened swamp, as this pair was, and not far from their spousal hollow.

The wind had turned up another notch by the time I crawled

into the tent. The flame inside the candle-lantern was quiet and steady, but the rest of the world shook and flapped and shivered. Unless a branch fell on the tent or the canoe, everything was secure, and after the long day on the water, the hours of opening vistas and broad perspectives, there was an immense comfort in the frail enclosure of the tent, and the page of my book in its pool of yellow light. Reading felt like a sacrament, an act having a mysterious value in itself, apart from the purport of what was written. What I thought didn't signify, rain or shine. The barred owls hooted and wailed in the intervals of sleep, pine needles pelted the tent, but no rain came.

Everything was still, and no stars were visible, when I got up, a little before day, ate my cold breakfast, and waited until there was light enough to get the canoe back down the steep bank and into the river. The air was saturated, and it seemed that any slight vibration would precipitate its moisture. The two wood-duck flushed and flew squealing away down river, alarmed as though they had just learned that today was the day that the sky would fall in sure enough. In the heavy, unnatural atmosphere of the morning, that felt like a reasonable supposition, but it did not come to pass.

Instead, the river presented a sleek, pearly surface, and the morning twilight lasted until nine or ten o'clock. A few miles below Bear Bluff, the Waccamaw enters a stretch called the Wild Horse, in which it seems to recollect its younger and friskier days, and twists with accelerated current through a series of sharp bends. It was deeper here than upstream, and you could sense a new power in its movement. As far as I know, this is the only section of the river that has ever earned a name for itself, and it seemed to me likely that it would have been the helmsman of a steamboat, or some rafter who went swimming here, who gave it its designation. Ascending the Wild Horse in a steamboat would have been like driving up a twisting mountain road: it would have been slow, but, if you had power enough, not particularly hazardous, especially since the boat would have been lightly loaded. But coming downriver from Red Bluff or above, with 100 or 150 tons of cargo, drawing six feet of water, would have been like going down the twisting mountain road, only more so. On a sharp turn, in a boat that would be 80 or 100 feet at the waterline, the upstream side would have lain across the current like a dam or boom, with the water piling up against it and forcing the vessel into the bank at the outside of the curve. With its big reversible wheels, located amidships and opposite each other, a river steamer was able to perform many of the same maneuvers that two canoeists use in white water. It could reverse one wheel, driving forward with the other to make a pivot turn on a sharp bend, or back-paddle with both wheels, while holding the stern at an angle to the current, in order to move the boat directly across stream, toward the inside of the curve; and then, at the right moment, the helmsman could apply full power forward to both paddles, to pull out of that bend and maneuver toward the inside of the next one. With enormous power at his disposal, the helmsman did not have to worry about being overmatched by the river, but he had little room for miscalculation, inattention, or second thoughts. Even the canoe, coming downstream with her light cargo of duffle, rations, and other more or less ponderable baggage, and drawing two or three inches of water, required some circumspection in the negotiation of the Wild Horse.

I would have given away a good deal of the history of my century for the chance to meet one of the steamers of the Waccamaw line pushing up river, taming the Wild Horse, on this glassy, silent morning. I was entering a section where the current of my own family's history ran strong; if I had met one of the boats of the Waccamaw line, the chances were one in three that she would have been the flagship, the *F. G. Burroughs*, which was named (like my father and so, at one remove, like me) for my great grandfather. But even in my father's youth, steamboats were on the way out. He had ridden on one—the *Mitchell C.*—exactly once. Because there had been only that one time, the details were vivid to him.

He and his mother had gotten aboard in Conway, to go down to Georgetown. He had his .22 rifle, and posted himself in the bow of the boat, where he could snipe at cooters and hope for a summer duck; he had roamed the big upper deck and watched the river slide by.

But my memory of his memory focusses on one detail about steamboat architecture that I have never heard mentioned, no doubt because steamboats flourished in an age when such details were unmentionable. For the higher class of passengers, who rented staterooms, there were the usual sanitary facilities—commodes with chamber pots. But for deck hands, day-trippers, and adventurous boys, there was a door at the top of one of the wheel housings. You entered it from the upper deck. Inside was what was in effect an outhouse. But what an outhouse! You sat in that shuddering, cavernous place, with the huge wheel churning and threshing beneath you, driving the heavy boat and, incidentally, serving you as a combination flush toilet and bidet. Daddy said that, to a small boy, it seemed like a throne of the gods. The splashing might have been unpleasant in the winter time, but in the summer it meant that you emerged refreshed and relieved. There was the clean, fresh smell of the river, and the sense of elemental powers below your seat. Emerson spoke disparagingly of travellers who could find nothing better to do with a quiescent volcano than bake their eggs in it, but he had never done it himself, and did not understand the human delight in finding a heroic solution to a negligible problem. There was a sublimity in the imagination that had conceived of using a wheel-house, and the whole vast mechanics of a steamboat, to serve this humble biological need; it was, Daddy said, akin to the instinct that had built the pyramids.

At the lower end of the Wild Horse, a bold bluff rises fifty or sixty feet above the river. This once was Grahamville, which had been a river port of some importance in the very modest scale of local commerce at the turn of the century. In addition to the inevitable turpentine still, there had been a cotton gin, a store, a post office, and a shed where cypress shingles were made. As turpentining operations went deeper into the hinterlands, a road eventually stretched due east from Grahamville through the bays and pine woods to the Atlantic Ocean, establishing a link between civilization and an isolated coastal community known as Cane Patch or Deep Head, well to the south of Little River. This road, no more than a set of wagon tracks through the sand, was superseded, in the first decade of this century, by the railroad, which came into Conway from the west, and then was extended eastward to the coast. Farsighted men, sensing commercial possibilities and knowing they would never be realized in a place called either Cane Patch or Deep Head, re-named this stretch of barren dunes, shrubby thickets, and swashes Myrtle Beach, and a tiny resort village began there—a few board-and–batten houses perched along the dunes. The first sanitation department consisted of a sow and her twelve pigs, who roamed the sandy streets and set a precedent for the irregular collection of garbage which outlasted them by many decades. The future greatness of Rome was also augured—less appropriately, some might say—by a sow and a litter of pigs. In Grahamville, ignorant of portentous developments to the east, one of my great-uncles took his first job as a clerk in the store. Eager, assiduous, and nervous, he came early to work on the first day, so he could memorize the price of everything in stock, and be ready to serve his customers with brisk efficiency. His first customer was an unintimidating little girl from a nearby farm. Her Mama had sent her to the store for two eggs' worth of lard, she said.

Now Grahamville could not even claim to be a ghost town. The river had lost its businesss to the railroad and the road; turpentining and cotton had played out; the store had closed and the post office had moved away. Not even a public landing remained. But this bluff was too high and handsome to be permitted a simple reversion to pines and oaks, and, beginning in the 1950s, a few people from Conway, decades ahead of their time, built summer houses along it. They eventually moved out to the river year round, becoming Conway's first commuters and initiating the gentrification of Grahamville. That process had continued and accelerated, and now I paddled beneath a residential neighborhood of quiet, prosperous-looking houses, each with its own dock or boathouse.

People were not up yet, and at this early hour of the morning the river took no notice of the suburb. On a long, wide reach just below Grahamville, an otter swam across the river ahead of me, raising a silver flange of wake. Wood-ducks flushed along the western, undeveloped bank, as wild and wary as their cousins upstream. A pair of them had infiltrated a flock of domestic mallards that puttered around the pilings of a dock, and they did not flush as I passed, but their watchful eyes never left me. An owl, ghostly as a snowflake in the gray stillness of the morning, drifted across the river, and I wondered if these creatures—the otter, the ducks, and the owl—might not in time become suburban status symbols, like one of Thomas Spivey's wishing wells or rustic benches. Pileated woodpeckers were here too, usually in pairs or trios. This morning they were playing aerial tag and arboreal peek-a-boo, chasing each other back and forth across the river or in tight opposed spirals up the boles of trees.

The twelve miles or so from Grahamville to Conway ought to have been familiar to me, but all along the east bank, wherever the land was high enough, there were new houses, many of them still in the process of construction. This disoriented me; I could not recognize the old landings and creek mouths that should have marked my progress and told me where I was. I paddled past lawns and houses that looked like upscale Potemkin villages to me, and I no doubt represented a sort of Rip Van Winkledom to them. Finally, about a mile above Conway, I came to Stilley Plywood, the only surviving lumber operation on the river. I had expected to find it either derelict and abandoned or modernized beyond recognition. But what I found was what I remembered, and what

I remembered had looked old, ramshackle, and jury-rigged even thirty years ago. It was a sprawl of unpainted, tin-roofed sheds and buildings beside the river; the muddy hulk of a barge was sunk along the waterfront. But steam was rising from the log-vat; and the air was full of the rusty creaking and whining of the crane that lifted the logs from the vat, and of the screeching of iron wheels against steel rails, as a tramcar shunted them to the mill. From the sound if its rickety racket, nothing had been changed, not even the oil. It was a strangely reassuring noise, deliberate, swaying, and antiphonic, punctuated by irregular clankings and the hissing expirations of steam. The crane hoisted a big gum log, gleaming wet and clouded with steam, from the vat, and swung it with sacerdotal gravity toward the tramway.

It has been a long time since Stilley's mill fished its logs from the Waccamaw, but I wanted to go up and have a look around. Grandmama Burroughs had gotten work here as an accountant after she had been left a widow with two sons to raise and educate, and I felt a sort of connection to this place. After she retired, she would always drive out to the mill at Christmas time, to deliver presents and speak to people, and as a child I would accompany her, not at all sure what it was that linked my Grandmother, a person whose dignity placed her immensely beyond the ordinary necessities of the human condition, to this untidy place. We would walk along gangplanks through the mud from one building to another; it would usually be a Friday afternoon, just before quitting time, and the swamps would encroach ominously on the mill in the winter twilight. When I walked in today, the office felt familiar. One or two window panes were missing, and the furnishings had the dusty, undistinguished antiquity of what you might find in an attic or a junk store.

I spoke briefly with the man I found inside. He could not tell me when Stilley's had ceased to rely on local hardwood; most of what they got now was sweetgum, from Virginia. It was made into low-grade veneers, to be used for the backs, bottoms, and drawers of inexpensive furniture. I had hoped I might look around the plant, and see the oversized lathe and blade at work, peeling veneer from the log the way you unroll paper towels from a cylinder. But I learned that safety regulations forbade my going through the mill unescorted, and so I picked my way past piles of sawdust, logs, and bark, and got back into the canoe. After all that I had seen along the river this morning, Stilley's had a comforting weight and solidity of association. I remembered how it would look when the river was high, and you would have needed a paddling boat to get around. But it had gone on functioning through all the fluctuations of the Waccamaw and the economy, as though it were simply a fact of local ecology.

By noon, I had passed under the trestle that carries the railroad east from Conway to Myrtle Beach. Bishop came upon the "country town of Conwayborough" about the same time of day, on the 19th of January, 1874. Conway was a fleeting glimpse for him: black stevedores on the docks, laughing and pointing at his strange little craft; the river, with the full force of the freshet behind it, swirling among the pilings. The little town behind its waterfront—the stately old Presbyterian Church, some plain and pleasant frame houses, a few storefronts along an unpaved street— could not have impressed him, if he saw it at all. I turned up Kingston Lake, paddled past church and churchyard and a municipal parking lot. Beyond these lay the modest grid of streets, scarcely changed from my boyhood, that constitutes downtown Conway. Across the lake from the parking lot somebody's trotlines were suspended from cypress twigs, and three of the twigs were swaying and bobbing lazily. I lifted each line with the paddle as I came to it, to discover what strange life was there. Two catfish and a cooter. The catfish looked to weigh a pound apiece, slate gray backs, pallid bellies, bulging eyes and soft, jawless mouths fixed in a minstrel's wide and hopeless smile. The garfish and mudfish that you might pull from these waters look primitive, but a catfish only looks embryonic, slack-bodied and unossified. By comparison to the catfish, the cooter—a big and ornery slider—seemed like a creature of my own kind. I cut the line as close to the hook as I could, and watched him swim with a scurrying motion back down out of sight. The hook would rust away in time. It had been baited, as trotlines frequently are, with a small cube of Ivory soap, so the turtle's wound would, I supposed, be disinfected.

For the first half mile above its confluence with the Waccamaw, the western bank of Kingston Lake is high, and, for reasons that would now seem aesthetic but once were purely practical, this has been, from the earliest days of the town, choice residential property. At the end of this stretch, the lake widens into what is in effect a small pond, then narrows sharply, takes a dogleg to the right, and enters the swamp. The last of the high ground, which is located on the corner and looks straight down the lake toward the Waccamaw, has always been called Snow Hill. Tradition says that a man named Snow was the original owner, and adds that he lies buried under a fine oak that stands at the corner of the property.

I pulled the canoe out at the foot of Snow Hill. The house there was undergoing tremendous renovation and expansion. It occurred to me that I would need to tell my children how the old Snow Hill house had looked, in the same way that my Grandmama Burroughs had told me how the house that had stood there before that had looked, and the same way that her mother-in-law could have told her what the house before *that* one had looked like. So much building on one site, by the generations of one family, ought to mean something, I thought, and promised myself I would think about it further. But first there was the business at hand. I unloaded the canoe and picked it up—an action which always makes you feel as proud and showy as Lazarus—and carried it across the street. Then went back and fetched up my gear, in two trips. As

I put the last of it down, Mama stuck her head out of the back door. "Well dog my cats," she said. "Just in time for lunch. Come right in this kitchen and wash your hands. But take off those boots before you do."

# 4   Snow Hill

After I came in, we went out to the porch and sat there, having a
ceremonial glass of sherry before lunch, talking about the river,
and looking across at Snow Hill and Kingston Lake. I was washed
up and bootless. "Improves you considerably," Mama said.

This was not the house I had grown up in, although I had spent
a great deal of time here as a child. It had belonged to my grandmother, Frances Coles Burroughs, who was known to her grandchildren as Real Frances. When she died in 1964, the house looked
like it might follow suit—the paint scaling, the roof bad, the yard,
overgrown and encroaching, threatening to submerge the whole
structure. It stood empty for better than two years, while Mama
and Daddy hesitated. Their last child had grown up and moved
out; Frances's house had more space than they needed, and, even
if it could be restored to health, it would be possessive in the way
that old houses are, continually demanding attention and expense.
I think too that Mama felt some of the reservations that almost
any married woman might feel about inhabiting a place haunted
by her mother-in-law. But they finally made the decision—sold
the neat and convenient single-story house they had built shortly

after their marriage, left its suburban neighborhood of mostly professional people of their own generation, and came back here, to where Daddy had been born.

The move pleased me deeply. Although my parents have renovated, modernized, and to that extent exorcised the house, the life and character of my grandmother survive inside it. As they have settled in here, they have also become grandparents, assuming for my children the status that Real Frances had for me: curators of a certain kind of mystery; evidence, like the house itself, of a continuity between the present and a past that, in the minds of children, shelves off very quickly into the realm of legend, fiction, and stark implausibility.

Across the road, Snow Hill was where my family's memory, if not its history, began. Beyond it, if you try to continue on up the lake, lie the swamps that, left to their own devices, so effortlessly swallow up all evidences of human enterprise. If you skirt the swamps, walking past Snow Hill and bearing northward through two or three backyards, you come to the cemetery. It is a small replica of Conway, with intersecting sandy lanes beneath big pines and sweetgums, the individual plots with their stones like the yards and houses of the town. Azaleas, camellias, tidy borders of daffodils—in the spring, it is a garden. Natural and human history converge—the trees and shrubs; the names and dates on headstones. During a funeral, you would hear the cry of a yellowhammer or the squeal of a wood-duck from the swamps. It is a pleasant place to walk, better than a park. Real Frances would sometimes bring me here, perhaps to tidy up Arthur's plot, and tell me a little bit about him, in her matter-of-fact way. Her past, which had not been easy, lived quietly in her.

Her house was always familiar to me, in the sense that I can no more recall my first experience of it than I can my first experience of my own house. But, at the same time, it always had a feeling of difference, and its physical features seemed to express a distinctive sense of time and purpose. My house felt as unlike it as a post

office feels like a church. Her house was cold in winter, and even in summer had a musty suggestion of coolness about it, like a cellar. There were big windows and glass-panelled doors, the porch ran all the way around the house, and at its edges grew shrubs and ornamental trees—the inevitable azaleas and camellias, crape myrtles, boxwood, yaupon, dogwood, holly, a fig. Indirect and filtered through branches and leaves, the light that came into the rooms filled them with a glaucous, underwater tranquility. The plaster was cracked, the varnish on the floor was nearly black with age, the furniture—or at least my favorite pieces of it—was sway-backed and spavined.

My feeling for her house had as its context my assumption that my parents, and the house they lived in, the routines they kept, defined the Real World. As far as I could see, Mama and Daddy administered, and were themselves governed by, an iron system of disciplines, rewards, and punishments. Although I had it on good authority that I lived in a land of freedom and opportunity, I also believed that maturity would be the fitting of myself to a vast, impersonal machine—an army that conscripted universally, and demanded the military virtues of stoicism, self-suppression, and anonymity. Daddy was a lawyer and, as I was later to learn, an exceptional one—learned, conscientious, acute, and of great probity. He dealt with the exact, complex finality of the law, and not all the loose talk that surrounded it. But as a child, I could not imagine how his profession might have afforded him any satisfaction, or expressed anything that was inside him. I could only see the austerity, monotony, and impersonality of it: the lawyerly gray suit that distanced him from affectionate familiarity; the punctual inevitability of his schedule, day in and day out, with no consideration of season or weather. I would sometimes hear him speaking into the dictaphone, pronouncing each syllable with an exaggerated, toneless precision. It sounded like one machine talking to another, in the idiom of Necessity that would soon claim me, and make me into what an adult had to be: a personification, deriving my authority and identity from Law or Science or Finance or Government.

But, if I gained from Daddy's official and professional self an image of what the Real World was and what it would require, I also saw in him—and was invited to see—remnants and vestiges of a reality besides the one he served. There was especially the hunting and fishing—as soon as he stepped into those clothes, something in him relented. We fished and hunted with great seriousness, and here too there were important codes and protocols to be observed, but these were the expressions and enlargements of a solemn happiness. They gave to hunting and fishing a strong quality of ritual, but not of obligation, regulation, or restraint. Almost every place we went had some story attached to it, some experience out of Daddy's own boyhood. There was a dimension of retrospection, even of re-enactment, to our expeditions. It was as though something from an earlier, less grim, historical dispensation could still be found, if you hunted hard enough, if you fished devoutly enough.

Real Frances and her house—I scarcely distinguished the two—belonged to this earlier dispensation, the remote, almost unimaginable time when my father had been a child. It, and she, were a sanctuary from the bleak reality I saw ahead of me. In its recesses, in her speech and calm, undemonstrative affection, I gained some sense of a world that antedated the one I inhabited, and that opened backwards, into larger and more adventurous possibilities than existed in any future I could possibly foresee. The simple business of daily life—going out to fetch a load of slab wood for her kitchen stove, and startling a big wood rat in the shed—led to discoveries. There were bats in the attic; in the late winter, with the returning warmth, lizards—the little ruby-throated anoles that we called chameleons, and, less commonly, a big, flat-headed, villainous-looking skink—would bask on the porch and steps, their eyes closed, their soft flanks pulsing slightly. The azaleas crowded in against the house like a jungle; the thick, muscular vines of wisteria quietly choked an elm. On still, frosty nights, you could snuggle down under covers, secure in the nest of bedding, and hear owls hooting from the Kingston Lake swamps. In the yard, Spanish moss draped the trees and made them ghostly and ancient.

The past, like the bats and the lizards, colonized the house and echoed from the neighboring houses, most of them belonging to people of Real Frances's generation, her in-laws and cousins by marriage. Inside, there were old books and portraits, but these were of no interest to a child. In the front hall, opposite the stairway, hung two muskets—one a smoothbore, the other an Enfield, the standard rifle of both armies in the Civil War—and a sabre. These were more promising. Upstairs there was a framed letter in the hallway, coming simply and directly out of the legendary history—a man, his daughter, his grandson:

Dear Fanny,

I send your lost boy home, to our great joy. He waked us up last night just as the clock struck twelve tired out and worn down. The Yankees have been trying to starve him, and have weak[en]ed and reduced him very much but thank God his limbs are all whole and sound. I hope all wars and bloodshed are over and that you may long keep him with you now and enjoy his society. I intended to come over with him, but that would compel him to walk, as I have but one horse; so I have concluded to send Ally with him to bring the mare back. Give my love to all and tell Eliza when she has a safe opportunity to send her *watch* over and I will make it run for her.

Your Father,<br>T. L. G. Green

28 June 1865

But the real sense of the past wasn't transmitted by her ancestral souvenirs and mementoes. It was woven into routines and rooted in yards. In the summer, I would wake early, go down into the kitchen, take the kettle, fill it, and slip out the kitchen door. Through the hedge, across Aunt Effie's yard, across Applewhite Lane, to Lucille's. The dew would be cold under my bare feet, and the air was full of a momentary sweetness, before the blighting heat of another summer day had settled over the neighborhood. There was a surreptitious pleasure, which I have never gotten over, at being out and abroad in the freshness of the world, while people of consequence still slept. You might see things you'd never expect to see in town—a rabbit nibbling and twitching nervously in the middle of a lawn; a pair of quail, followed by their chicks, scurrying all in a row down Applewhite Lane.

Lucille's pump stood in her backyard. I'd prime it, pouring the tapwater in the kettle down its throat, then pump: first a dry, hopeless creaking until the leathers moistened and the suction took hold; then the solid resistance to the handle, the gargling in the pipe, and the water sloshing up. Real Frances had taught me to hold my hand across the pump's muzzle and let the water build up behind it until it overflowed. That was the way to be sure that there were no air pockets in the pipe, no discontinuities between myself, standing with the sun just beginning to touch the top branches of the big pecan tree above me, and what the Bible called the waters under the earth. That simple mechanism, and the sudden gush of water out of the iron snout of the pump, was for me the first pastoral, the stylized acting out of a simple necessity.

I would fill the kettle to take it back over. Real Frances had no shortage of water in her house, but it was town water: artesian, slick and soft against the palate, and, in her judgment, unfit for the making of coffee. And the making of coffee, in a four-cup, wineglass-stemmed percolator that rattled and spat and vibrated on the stove like the Little Rocket that Couldn't, was her inflexible custom, carried out with strict precision. It was to be done in such a way at such a time, and it was to be done with fresh pump water, from Lucille's.

Lucille's house was the oldest in the neighborhood, and perhaps the oldest in town. It had been the original house at Snow Hill, and was small and neat, as she was herself. She was Frances's sister-in-law, but the two of them seemed like natural sisters, easy and offhand in each other's company. And, except for Real Frances, she was my favorite antediluvian relative. She would be up early, hear the pump, and stick her head out the back door, with some message for me to carry back—something about altar flowers, or news about somebody's health. Perhaps because she had been the youngest of a large family, she had a quick rapport with children, and liked to tell stories from her own childhood, back when the railroad ran the unpaved length of Main Street, there were no cars, steamboats were a daily excitement, and Conway, South Carolina, was a boy's paradise, on the order of Hannibal, Missouri. My grandfather Arthur had been her favorite brother, and she would tell me about his escapades, including the one I liked best, the story of the Horse that Wasn't Afraid of Trains.

Real Frances talked less about the past. She had grown up in Danville, Virginia, where family history was a serious business, and had not moved to Conway until she was eighteen, so the town had no magic of childhood association for her. She was also less of a raconteur by nature than Lucille, and much more of a

107

listener. Inspired by Daddy's and Lucille's stories, I would invent stories of my own—my exploits in the South Pacific during the Second World War, or an alligator that had, that very morning, rushed up out of the lake, run down a stray dog, caught and eaten it before my eyes. She would pay me a grave attention and say little; nothing stops an amateur liar so effectively as noncommittal silence. On pleasant afternoons we might walk down to the lake and there—cane poles, can of worms, and all—make a solemn pretense at fishing. She would sometimes point out to me the things that weren't there. This had been where the cotton gin was; the wharf where the steamboat docked was here. Just along the shore of the lake ran the sawdust road. It had continued out into the swamps and up to a bridge, crossed the lake and there, directly opposite us, terminated at Arthur's mill. At freshet time, the road would simply float away, but it could quickly be rebuilt— mills always produce more sawdust than they know what to do with. She would point over to where the mill had stood; she had been able to see it from her front porch. Now it was all just swamp; even in my childhood, you'd have needed a team of archaeologists, armed with machetes, to find any remnant of it. Frances was precise; she and Daddy were similar in that regard, and also in their scrupulous preserving of topographic history—boundaries, buildings, where roads had run, the lay of the land and the uses it had been put to.

I learned about Snow Hill and my family slowly, unsystematically, and by osmosis, about the same way that children learn to talk. Later, thinking that my own children might one day be curious about it, I did a little reading and asked a few questions, to bridge gaps and fill in blanks. Family tradition was something like the river—parts of it I knew very well, and other parts more remotely, by hearsay twice removed. But it was not long or intricate enough for me to get seriously lost.

My great-grandfather had bought Snow Hill shortly after the Civil War. During the war, it had had distinguished tenants: the

household of Plowden Weston, a Georgetown rice planter, secessionist, and certainly one of the richest and most powerful men in
South Carolina. He owned four plantations—Waterford, Hagley,
Weehawka, and True Blue—in the prime rice country of the lower
Waccamaw, on both sides of the river. His principal dwelling, at
Hagley, was routinely described as princely. These holdings were
vulnerable to Federal gunboats, and he needed a secure place to
stow his family, slaves, and other movable property until the war
was over.

Weston's wife was English, an expression of his own intense
Anglophilia, and she had recently acquired, as a companion and
a sort of domestic overseer, a genteel Englishwoman named Elizabeth Collins, who left a simple narrative of her experiences
(*Memories of the Southern States*, Tauton, 1865). "Towards the end of
January, 1862," she writes, "Mrs. W. made up her mind to visit
Conwayboro, a country town (if such a place could be called a
town) where she had been informed was a cottage that was likely
to suit her." It was a difficult trip by carriage, "through a rough
country, full of the stumps of trees, and roads of very deep sand,"
and the journey, of less that forty miles, took all day, and was
completed by torchlight. Elizabeth Collins and Mrs. Weston slept
in the house of Captain Pope. "The next morning came, and off
we went to view the intended new home, Snowhill, which was
very pleasantly situated on a bluff, and nicely sheltered by a grove
of elm trees. The number of rooms was very small to that of Hagley house; however, Mrs. W. was pleased with the look of the
cottage, and agreed to rent it for the sum of a hundred and twenty
dollars a year. The out-houses, stable, etc were very much out of
repair."

Renty, the black carpenter, was sent up to put things in order,
and flats—scows normally used for transporting men, animals, and
the rice their labor produced to and from the fields—were loaded
with plate, silver, china, rugs, the most precious of the furnishings
of Hagley, and all of the books from Weston's library, which was
famous. Slaves poled the flats up the Waccamaw: first the land-

scape of diked fields and low, wide horizons which constituted the known world for most of them, then pushing up into Horry, entering a river now flowing black and sparkling, not brown and turbid like the one they knew, although it was all the same river. The river narrowed, trees closing in ahead of them, as they labored on, and finally came to Conway. Prince, a coachman, registered a dismay which Elizabeth Collins completely shared: "Conwayboro looks like the last place God made."

Plowden Weston had raised and outfitted a company at the outset of the war; it became Company A of the 10th South Carolina Volunteers. He went off to Corinth, Mississippi, as its captain. Sentimental novels of the plantation South make the lives of Mrs. Weston and Elizabeth Collins, left behind in Conwayboro, almost too easy to visualize: two women alone in a house, enduring the material and emotional deprivations of war, and slowly, resisting it with all their powers of faith, hope, and delusion, coming to the realization that the war was being lost.

Elizabeth Collins was wholly, stridently and almost religiously Southern in her sympathies and outlook. One senses in her a conventional and unreflective woman, removed from the social cosmos that defined her, and fixing all her hopes for its restoration on the maneuvering of distant armies. Hagley, with its ordered life and clear sense of social hierarchy, was, for all its strangeness, an outpost of Englishness; her own Englishness there would have conferred upon her a semi-aristocratic status, even though her duties were distinctly menial. Conwayboro was something altogether different. Women smoked pipes, yet spoke to her and even to Mrs. Weston in terms of complete familiarity, as though they knew no other manner of address. At her best, she could see something decent in these unlikely neighbors: "I used to think them a rough lot of people, but their manner showed they were very kind." But they jeopardized her beleaguered sense of her own dignity and station. She needed companionship—her relations with Mrs. Weston seem to have been civil, and not intimate—but not of the sort that Conway could provide. She used to visit Mrs. Ludlum, "who was a neighbor, but a very talking woman, and would sometimes give me more uneasiness than she did pleasure." When Elizabeth Collins would, in the most conventional and accepted way, ask a female acquaintance how she was, the standard answer would be "Mighty bad," followed by a litany of medical complaint. Religion was no consolation. There was no Episcopal congregation, so she was obligated to consort with nonconformists. "I think the Methodist church will beat any church I ever saw for disorder and dirt." People sat in the pews without distinction of rank; every third or fourth seat contained a spittoon, "and I have no doubt but the pulpit contains another."

Plowden Weston's health failed him and forced his retirement from active service. He was briefly in Conway at the end of 1862, but was soon taken off by new duties—he was elected Lieutenant Governor, and that job, and trying to keep Hagley and his other holdings in some kind of shape, allowed him little time with his family. He rejoined them for a last time in September 1863. Tuberculosis was far advanced; breathing had become a labor that would soon exhaust him. He spent his last months at Snow Hill; when the weather and his health permitted, he would go for brief outings in a carriage, and must have found little enough to look at in this poor place, which had only the haziest comprehension of his greatness. He might as well have been dying in exile. The end came in January of 1864. His body was taken downriver on a flat, and buried at All Saints' Church, not far from Hagley, among his own people and class. Within a year, Elizabeth Collins and Mrs. Weston made their way to Wilmington, North Carolina, waited for a moonless night, and ran the blockade, back to England. Neither ever set foot in the New World, much less Horry County, again.

For the two Englishwomen, Conway must have been a kind of apparition, a world they could scarcely permit themselves to see, any more than they could permit themselves to see the harsh realities of the ricefields or, for that matter, of the streets of nine-teenth-century London. And Conway must have found the Westons to be apparitions of another sort—the people with all that cargo of wealth and power and scarcely conceivable privilege coming up the river, inhabiting the old Snow place, yet never properly becoming neighborly, preserving always a certain air of banished royalty. And then departing abruptly and completely, disappearing back downriver, leaving behind them only the alluring and persistent mirage of the baronial South.

The ignorant, rustic neighbors of Elizabeth Collins and Mrs. Weston, and the underdeveloped little hamlet they inhabited, were as much a reflection of the plantation system as the princely establishment at Hagley, with its big house, its tidy street of slave quarters, its mill, its splendid library and wine cellar, and its miles and miles of laboriously reclaimed, meticulously cultivated, and staggeringly productive ricefields. But, in Conway and elsewhere, thinking along these lines has never proceeded very far. When the private world of the planter—the lavish superfluity of manners and courtesy, the hard, adventurous, hospitable life that seems in retrospect like something out of Tolstoy—all went to smash, its economic substructure and rigid exclusivity were forgotten. In sentimental memory, which is a form of amnesia, the plantation culture floated free from the damage it did, not only to the slaves who were its direct victims, but to the whole huge class of white farmers and backwoodsmen who existed at its fringes. The planters' wealth did not create markets or jobs for them; it did not found the cities, schools, or even mills in which they might have come together and gained some sense of social cohesion. But in the aftermath of the war, the plantation became a sort of New Jerusalem: a vision rising out of history as a compensation for history. Every white Southerner could feel himself disenfranchised by the war from his rightful enjoyment of that felicity. And even before the war, backwoodsmen of energy and ambition generally dreamed of enfranchisement within the planter class, and not of opposition to it. The next proprietor of Snow Hill, F. G. Burroughs, was such a backwoodsman.

He came from the other direction—from the hard poverty of a small farm in Martin County, North Carolina. As edited and augmented by his descendants, his story begins like a folktale: one day, breaking new ground for planting, he stumps his toe, swears, throws down the plough, and announces, on the spot, that he will die or be damned before he'll spend another day behind a mule. It was 1857; he was twenty-two years old, unmarried, and full of hardihood. There were no doubt maternal tears and fatherly counsel as he enacted the recurrent scene of his region, his class, his century: the Young Man off to Seek His Fortune in the Great West. His ambition was as stark and simple as Thomas Sutpen's: to own a hundred slaves, and to own them before he was much older.

His plan was to go to Tennessee (an ambition he must have reflected upon wryly when he eventually got there, five years later), all the way out to Memphis, where he had an uncle who spoke of the fine prospects in that vicinity. But there was a mysterious kinsman closer at hand. A year or two earlier, his father had been down into the gloomy forests of northern Horry as a drover, delivering supplies and hired slaves to a turpentining operation, quite possibly that of Colonel D. W. Jordan. While there he heard of a Jim Burroughs, who was said to be from Martin County, but who had lived for a good many years in Conwayboro, and had become a man of some estimation there. The father suspected he knew who Jim Burroughs was, and suggested that his son first go that way and look him up, before heading on out to Tennessee.

The father's suspicions were right. Jim Burroughs was no Burroughs at all, although his wife was. She was F. G. Burroughs's aunt, his father's sister. Her husband's real name was Jim Pulley, and he had killed a slave in Martin County and abruptly disappeared, leaving her and at least one child behind in the process.

Apparently Conwayboro was remote enough; he settled there and prospered, occasionally sending money or goods back to the wife in North Carolina, but never encouraging her to follow him. Perhaps she did not desire to.

Pulley was a man of expansive and flexible temperament, not to say a scoundrel. He took a second wife in Conway, without notifying the first, whom he continued to subsidize. There were additional children by this second marriage, but his appetite for connubiality was apparently insatiable, and so he took a black mistress, living openly with her in Conway. This union, too, was fruitful, and Pulley's will would eventually make provision for what he called "my ill-begotten children of color." He would finally die in reduced circumstances, having outlasted his wives and living an old man's life as a supernumerary in the household of one of his children, down in Georgetown. He wanted to be buried in Conway, but the teamster who was transporting his body lost control of the horse at Yauhannah Ferry, on the Pee Dee. The horse plunged off the ferry; horse, wagon, and the mortal remains of Jim Pulley were swept down the river. The teamster was black. Nobody has ever suggested that he knew of the murder back in North Carolina, or that he had deliberately goaded the horse; but it was felt that the teamster was, nevertheless, the agent of that Justice which Jim Pulley fled and flouted so wantonly and for so long.

But that was all to come. Late in 1857, when my great-grandfather arrived in Conway to seek out his kinsman, he found him to be a man of affairs, in the public, as well as the private, realm. He owned a turpentine still and a store, and was the sheriff, no less, of Horry County. From this distance, the whole thing—the single-minded and grimly determined young adventurer arriving in a hamlet lost in the middle of swamps and bays; the casually polygamous, physically indolent, hospitable, and occasionally homicidal sheriff there to greet him, and turning out to be his uncle, although not the uncle he had originally set out to find—

suggests a world and an ethos that lie somewhere between Yok-napatawpha and Macondo. If F. G. Burroughs felt any resentment towards this prosperous blackguard, who had used his aunt so shabbily even as he was appropriating her maiden name (and living in a way not calculated to enhance its respectability), he did not show it. He would later give advice to his son which he himself had perhaps followed in his dealings with Pulley: "Never tell all you nowe. Find out all you can, and lay it a way and use it when to your advantag. . . . Never use your friends [i. e. relatives] to much. Call on them when you can doe no other way. The more times you call on them, the more times you will be called on."

Pulley apparently was pleased to meet the young man who knew his real name and the secret that lay behind it; in any event, he was remarkably kind to him, and family tradition has never so much as whispered that his generosity might have been inspired by actual or implicit blackmail. In a gesture that was, I suppose, the equivalent of laying a sword on great-grandfather's shoulder and proclaiming him a knight, Pulley made his young kinsman a deputy sheriff, and then set about helping him get established in the town. F. G. Burroughs quickly acquired the principal interest in a turpentine still and a small store, probably using capital or credit supplied by his uncle. He took whatever jobs turned up— almost his first recorded act in Conway was to bid on a public works project. His bid was low, and he completed the project to the municipality's satisfaction, although his uncle, if he were an imaginative man, might have contemplated it with some uneasiness: a gallows.

Great-grandfather found a partner to tend the store—first a man named Gurganus, then, after his death, Hampton Hart. That gave him time to mind the turpentine still and to begin inspecting the quality and quantity of the pinelands around Conway. It is natural to suppose that, in this pleasant community, with the prospect of a moderately prosperous, reasonably comfortable life ahead of him, he abandoned his grandiose dream, to own a hundred slaves before he was thirty. But nothing about his character or subsequent career suggests that this was the case. If he decided to settle in Conway it was because he deemed it compatible with his ambition. And if he saw his fortune there, he must have seen it in the pine forests. He came from a region where turpentining had been carried on much longer and much more intensively than in Horry, and possibly understood better than another man might how much unexploited wealth was still there in the woods around Conway. The county was underpopulated and undeveloped. The railroad, which Bishop had called "one of the great mediums of enlightenment to mankind," and which was the century's supreme emblem of progress and prosperity, hadn't yet reached Conway or any other portion of Horry County, and such roads as existed were scarcely more than wagon tracks. If a man were resolute, and willing to gamble on the future, the region's backwardness was its greatest asset.

And then, of course, the war came. Great-grandfather enlisted as a private in the Brooks Guard, soon to become Company B of the 10th South Carolina. He certainly would have known by sight Captain Weston, of Company A, and, given the informality of the military hierarchy in the Confederate armies, he might have exchanged a few words with him, as one recent citizen of Conway to another. But Weston was one of the many who were weeded out by disease, exposure, and privation. The member of the officer class who most impressed great-grandfather was clearly not Weston but his regimental commander, Arthur Middleton Manigault.

Great-grandfather seems to have talked very little about his wartime experience. The captain of his company spoke of him as an exemplary soldier, one who was repeatedly urged to accept a commission, but who refused to do so, and remained in the ranks until the end. The war he saw was as bad as war could be. Up until the Battle of Franklin, when the regiment was shattered (he was captured in this fiasco; Manigault was severely wounded), the brigade of which he was a part never had an effective strength of more than 2,500 men, and prior to its last battle, it had sustained 2,700 casualties in combat. To these must be added the large but unspecified number who died or were disabled by disease. The odds did not favor survival.

We know, at least in the abstract, how terrible the dying was in that war, yet most first-person accounts of it are curiously detached, focussing on issues of generalship and maneuver, accepting the horror of it as though that were only incidental, like mosquitoes on a camping trip. ("The Lieutenant commanding the rifle section was unfortunately killed as he was returning to his command," writes Manigault in his memoirs, "a rifle cannon shell cutting him in two.") Perhaps because this was a war written about so extensively by its generals, and perhaps for more complicated reasons, having to do with the need that each side felt to make it, retroactively, into a crusade, we hear very little about its stress and trauma, combat fatigue, shell shock; very little about what its survivors may have suffered. Anything about my great-grandfather's war must be inferred from his silence, from his refusal to accept promotion, and from the fact that, for three years, from middle Tennessee to Chickamauga, and on the long, stubborn retreat to Atlanta, and then back again into Tennessee, with Hood's disastrously misconceived, blundering campaign against Nashville, and from there to Fort Douglas, Illinois, and the prisoner's life of disease, dirt, cold, and semi-starvation, he kept the soapdish and shaving mirror of one Jessie Boyd. Boyd had died of wounds in the retreat from Murfreesboro, and had bequeathed his shaving tackle to great-grandfather, who buried him beside the road in the only way he could in that harsh, frozen country— wedged his body into a rocky cleft and piled stones over it. The dish and mirror he eventually willed to his daughters, as memorials of things he seems to have been unable to forget or discuss.

Manigault, his commander, was a Georgetown county rice

planter, scion of an illustrious Charleston family. He was also a West Point man, a stickler for drill and discipline. Whatever chance there was for victory in the west was lost at Chickamauga, through the almost psychotic irresolution of Bragg, and Manigault knew it, but he kept his command together, tolerated no grumbling or relaxing of standards, and provided my great-grandfather with an example, if he needed one, of organization, enterprise, and pertinacity. When I read Manigault's memoirs, trying to get a sense of my great-grandfather's military career, what struck me was the attitude towards the enlisted men. Manigault tended them and used them and valued them precisely as a drover would his horses. Or, of course, a planter his slaves. Before Chickamauga, they were rested and fit, in fine fettle. He looked at them as they passed by in "the steady, swinging stride peculiar to the Army of Tennessee," their clothing tattered and their spirits high: "It was impossible to behold their physical condition and development, and their ruddy cheeks browned by exposure, without a feeling of admiration and satisfaction. . . . What splendid condition! What hardihood! Nothing but bone, sinew, and muscle! Not a pound too much of flesh!"

In return, he had from his soldiers the kind of respect that goes to the stern and unsparing taskmaster. He knew my great-grandfather and called him by his first name, a mark of special distinction. After the war, he returned to his fine Palladian home at White Oak, his plantation on the North Santee River, and tried to resume the life of a planter, but that life had passed. He eventually went into politics, and was three times elected Adjutant and Inspector General for the State of South Carolina. There is no record of any communication between him and his former soldier; the distance between Conway and the rice country was still greater than geography alone would suggest. But when my great-grandfather's ill-fated fourth son was born, in 1881, he remembered his old commander, and named him Arthur Manigault Burroughs.

Franklin Gorham Burroughs himself was discharged from prison and sent by train as far as Greensboro, North Carolina. From there, sick and malnourished, he made his way home on foot, a long journey through a countryside full of fear, with every stranger a potential enemy. Judging from the aftermath, he lost no time when he got back to Conway; he modified his ambition and resumed its pursuit as briskly as though he were returning from a long and restorative vacation.

The rest of his life was the realization of his ambition. Toward the end of it, he wrote to his eldest son, trying to distill all that he had lived through and learned into platitudes and useful maxims, words to live by: "Have prid enough to say to your selfe I WILL DOE—not I will try—but say I WILL, with the helpe of the Lord, be a man that my parents and county and state will not be a shame of. Have prid enough not to let no one from this county be a head of you." He goes on, and the voice of the soldier—not the officer but the private—comes out: "Nevr tell your teachr a storie. Nevr report any one if you can helpe it. Doe your duty when able. If a bad job is a head, dont go on sick list to keep out of it. Doe every thing like you are told. . . . Goe to the Front, Press Forward, Push a Head—dont waite because others doe. Press forward, and win the Prise."

His was a complicated ethos, one that combined a strong regard for duty and obedience with an insistence on initiative, will, and the necessity for risk. If the war taught him the foot soldier's code— prudence, a loyalty to one's comrades in the face of one's superiors and in the face of hardship—it also taught him, perhaps through the negative examples of the hapless Bragg and the headstrong Hood, the need for calculated, decisive, conclusive action. Somehow it all fused into a kind of final, apocalyptic sense: "When you start some thing git thrugh with it befor you stop. You will have a time for all thes things and be ready to meet them when the Hour and Minut comes. The time is now comin when evry minut is to be accounted for. Its all laid down and must be complid with." By 1886, he had established the Burroughs and Collins

Company, borrowed money, and begun shipping turpentine north. He was far better positioned than the overlords of the ricefields downriver. Horry, isolated and left to its own benightedness by the plantation economy, had some commercial connections to New York, as a result of the turpentine trade. The Captain of great-grandfather's company, W. J. Tolar, had a son, J. R. Tolar, who had spent the war with the Confederate commissary department. He learned a great deal, and after the war he moved quickly. He joined great-grandfather's former partner, Hampton Hart, and the two of them moved to New York, to establish themselves as Tolar and Hart, commission merchants.

This provided F. G. Burroughs with a line of credit. Fortune favored him. Almost as an afterthought, he insured his first shipment of turpentine; the ship sank, the insurance paid off, and he was still afloat. The Franco-Prussian War, which drove the price of naval stores to unprecedented heights, came at just the right time, when he was ready to expand. In the aftermath of the Civil War, money was scarce and there were few able-bodied men to work the land. Instead of leasing turpentining rights, as was customary, he found he could often buy the land outright for very little more. Still believing in the future, he correctly foresaw that when the turpentining had played out, the timber would remain, and would be in demand. He built turpentine distilleries throughout the county, frequently combining them with stores, which extended credit, took mortgages, and further enlarged his holdings. By the time the railroad finally came to Conway, in 1887, he was thriving, and was prepared to take advantage of the county's agricultural potential.

He married in 1866. He lived in a practical culture, and was a good judge. His advice to his son on the choosing of a wife could apply, with very little modification, to the choosing of a brood mare: "select you a good healthy woman for a wife. . . . Find out as much about the girl as you can befor marying, and alowing yourself to love her. See the family is all right, healthy and strong—no consumption and such like in the family. If that be the case, you will sooner or later expect some of your sones and daughtrs will have it too." His wife, Adeline Cooper, was better educated than he was; while he was off soldiering, she had two years at the Spartanburg Female Academy, in the upper part of the state, and then returned home and taught school at Cool Spring, a community west of Conway. Her prose is a good deal more presentable than his, and she had some sense of humor. In 1896, she wrote her daughter Lella, describing her husband's pleasure in a new artesian well that he had had dug at Snow Hill: "Papa says tell you he thinks as much of his well as he would of a good mule, and a good mule comes next to me with him, so you can imagine how much he likes it."

In 1867 he bought Snow Hill and began his family. Eventually there would be eleven children, eight of whom survived infancy. By 1881 the house no longer sufficed. He moved it about a quarter mile to the northwest, and it eventually was deeded to his youngest daughter, my great-aunt Lucille, from whose well I would draw water for my grandmother in the early coolness of summer mornings. In its place he built a big frame house, two and a half stories, with a single-story ell extending out the rear.

I know this Snow Hill house only from photographs and descriptions: high-ceilinged, airy, and facing to the north, to make it as cool as possible. It was not a planter's house, not a building to evoke European architecture. It was designed for a hot climate, but otherwise bore a strong resemblance to a large and prosperous New England farmhouse. All of his children would recall it as a place of abundant bustle: there was a slaughterhouse and a smoke house; an ice house (filled with New England ice, used as ballast by schooners coming down to pick up naval stores or lumber, and lightered up to Conway from Pott's Bluff); a cooling house, through which ran water from his fine artesian well; a grist mill; a wine-press; a pack house; barns; stalls; and, by the lake, a wharf and a cotton gin. There were always guests; meals were huge affairs; and the procuring, preserving, and preparing of food was a more or less incessant activity, through all the hours of the day and all the seasons of the year. Even after he had died and his children had grown up, Snow Hill remained an active place—in late summer, the mules and wagons lined up along the lakefront, bringing cotton to be ginned, and then a steamboat would maneuver up to the wharf to take it off. My father, as a child, found something elemental and troubling about Snow Hill. His most vivid memory is of the pig-killing in the winter—the squealing of the pigs, fire, smoke, and a big iron cauldron full of boiling water. To a boy raised more bookishly than any of his cousins, it all evoked hell-fire and damnation, and the fates of innocent young princes in Dickens's *Child's History of England*.

The letter from which I have been quoting was written by F. G. Burroughs to his eldest son, who had just gone off to a military academy in North Carolina, to acquire the education his father never had and never needed. The letter, full of parental counsel, no doubt contains less than the truth of his experience, but it is the closest thing to self-revelation that he left behind him. He was sitting in the house alone, so it must have been late at night. "Deare Sone," he begins:

> 33 years agoe today I left my natif state, Father, Mother, Brother & sisters. It seems very plaine to me now. . . . I had a purpose in my harte to doe something for my selfe. I could see others prosperd in thir world[ly] goods, and I detirmed to try and doe so.
>
> When I left home it was in slavry time. I left with the determation of owning 100 negros if I lived till 30 years old. Still I have lived till nearly 56 and dont own none.
>
> Of couse things changed by the war. I then had to make a nother start and effort for which I have no reason to complane. My sucess so far has bin owing to my energy and Promptness in my bussness transactions. I have allwase made it a Point to let my word be my

bond. When I promased a man to doe anything, I did it. But allwase tried to be very cearfull what I promasd.

What follows is perhaps suggested by his orthography—a mixture of the conventional and the improvised. It sounds to me as though he had read, or had read to him, Bunyan: "The right road is strate and as long as a man's life is. We doe not goe far on this long strate road before it forks off. A big plane road turnes off to the left, 4 times as wide looks like. It is paved with gold. That is wimen." He goes on at impressive length about the dangers of women, but it all sounds the way it sounds when I talk to my children about the dangers of drugs: a lurid denunciation of an evil known only through alarming reports and dire warnings. I doubt that Horry County, or Martin County, or the Army of the Tennessee had the necessary infrastructure to support his vision of depravity: "Wimen will most be certan to cary you to a bar room and from there, to the card table, and from there, to the Lawers office, and from there, to the corte House, and from there, to the jale, and the jale, to the gallos."

But set against this kind of more or less immemorial and generic advice of fathers to sons, is advice that plainly reflects his own observations and deductions. In addition to women, whiskey, and gambling, "a nother very importan matter ruins so many men, is publick life. Doe not hold no office no higher than overseer of the road. Keep out of Politicks." His affection for his son, and for his other children and the household he had established was perhaps conventional, but it was also strong. He knew that each child would one day look back to childhood "and say what a Good time I had arond Snowhilll, and I passed the Golden hours ther, but did not nowe it then." He saw the family as the chief source of happiness: "all we look on, after we are maried, is our family. That is the most to us of any thing, our wife and little ones."

But he was preparing his son for the practical life, and much of the practical life is a reducing of things, a forcing of them into simple and manipulable terms. It does not linger over textures, subtleties, intricacies. F. G. Burroughs wanted his son to prosper as he had; he did not particularly care whether he became more civilized, more cultured, or more sophisticated than the county of his birth. Great-grandfather's vision of life, of spiritual discipline, was consciously and deliberately that of his own private past, and not of the larger past. He was the soldier who had refused to become an officer, the boy who had sweated behind a mule. The country around him—the small farms, the lives that were self-sustaining, if only at a level of subsistence—was still the touchstone. He urged his son to "keep company with the best" in his free time; "but remembr your living comes out of the poor clas. If You do any busness, nevr cheat. Give wate and measur. Allways remembring the wate and measur will be returned the same to you, or to your offspring." Weight and measure take on the sense of an ultimate justice. That justice did not require him to remain one of the poor class, but it did require him never to forget his origins there, never to live as though his comfort was unconnected to its affliction. "I will pay for your scholing for 18 months," he sternly tells his son, "while a grate many don't have that done for them. Remembr it cost me over 8 dollars a day to send you ther."

Arthur Manigault Burroughs was his fourth son (two of them had died in infancy), and the first child to be born in the new house at Snow Hill. Looking at it now, it seems that, among all the children, he inherited the most of his father's venturesomeness and independence of spirit, and least of his prudence and hard practicality. But that is surmise—his life exists only in anecdotes, the things that his wife and siblings chose to preserve and repeat about him after he was dead. The style of their recollection was affectionate and indulgent: he was the Man Who Loved Trains. His life for me consisted of a series of scenes, almost like tableaux. Each involved a story that I had heard so often—and so often requested to hear—that it came to seem like a sort of dramatic skit, part of a regular repertoire or cycle—the Passing of Arthur:

- He is kneeling in the parlor at family prayer, not hearing the visiting preacher who drones on, hearing instead the whistle and the clash of couplings. He slips out of the room at a moment when all heads are bowed, all eyes devoutly closed, and races in his nightshirt out into the cotton field, where he can see across the withered stalks the headlamp, the sparks from the stack, and the dull orange of smoke reflecting the fire in the boiler—a night train coming into Conway. He stands enraptured through all the frantic calling for him, until he is found, hauled back inside and sent supperless to bed, having already given precocious indication that it is not his father's business he will be about.
- At seventeen or eighteen, at night again, he is again standing outside, this time beneath his youngest sister's window, furtively calling up to her. He had been sent off to the agricultural college at Clemson, much against his wishes; had run off to Atlanta, to try to enroll himself at Georgia Tech, where he could study engineering. Failing, had simply gone AWOL for a while, and now is back, an unrepentant prodigal. Lucille smuggled him into the house that night. "A delightful surprise for me," she used to say of his unexpected homecoming, "but not, the next morning, for Mama."
- A year or two later, costumed as honorary conductor aboard the "Black Maria" as it pulls the first train from Conway to Myrtle Beach. It is a small logging engine, runs on a wooden tramway, has only open flatcars—women passengers sit in chairs and carry parasols, to ward off sun, soot, and cinders—and stops to take on firewood every ten miles. But it is the future, and he is the man to summon all aboard.
- Solemnly shaking hands with his brothers, having just sold them his share in the family business. He will use the money to build

the sawmill on the other side of the lake. The future lies with lumber, not turpentine. And, to bring lumber to the mill, a whole network of railroads could be developed.

• In New York, with Real Frances. He has heard that the city is replacing its system of elevated trains with subways, and figures that this is an opportunity to get rolling stock on the cheap. Which, after considerable inspection and shopping around, he does—two little Forney locomotives and two coaches. Real Frances used to laugh at the memory: "I was the first bride in the history of the world to spend her honeymoon in a round-house."

• Lying on his back, in the middle of Main Street. In the background, wildly plunging, the Horse that Wasn't Afraid of Trains. Every horse in Conway was scared witless by the train that came down Main Street; Grandfather wanted one of more advanced views, and had this one shipped down to him from the North. He had watched with satisfaction as it came out of the box-car as calmly as a mule coming out of a barn. He mounted; the whistle blasted and the cars banged and screeched into motion: the horse was steady as a statue. And then, half-way home, it went beserk, and Arthur Manigault Burroughs lies on his back, proud owner of the only horse in Horry County that has a violently phobic and, as it turns out, incurable aversion to the sight, smell, and sound of pigs. A few weeks later, still in a condition of unsuppressed hysteria, the horse is blind-folded, railroaded into the box-car and sent back to whatever swineless place it had come from. Shortly after, Grandfather buys the first automobile in Conway.

• On his way to the mill, something of a dandy on horseback, fine leather gauntlets on his hands. Each morning, he goes over before breakfast, sees that everything is operating smoothly, then returns, along the sawdust road, to have a breakfast (no doubt including strong black coffee, made from well water) with his wife. But this morning he will pause to rake sawdust out from under the big saw; the gauntlet catches in the log carriage and his right arm is pulled in and mangled. He is carried back to the house, nearly dead from shock, and the arm is amputated in the front parlor.

- Standing, one sleeve empty now, his story growing more sombre, watching his two sons, aged four and two, happily at play in the yard. Instead of a tricycle or wagon, each has his own loco-motive and coal car, made of wood, with wheels, connecting rods, boilers, and fittings of iron; an iron track with wooden crossties runs over a considerable portion of the lawn. Perhaps it is play for him too, overlooking this miniature railway sys-tem, and still imagining (as his father had once imagined the plantation with the hundred slaves) a network of tramlines run-ning out from his mill into the uncut depths of Horry, bringing in logs and profit, spreading enlightenment, progress, and prosperity.

- Lying, terribly burned, on the foredeck of the *F. G. Burroughs* as she noses into the wharf below Snow Hill. He would, for a second time, be carried across the road unconscious, and be attended to in the front parlor. He regained consciousness once, to ask for water.

That is about all I know. And, because there is no longer any living memory of him (Daddy was four when Arthur died; he has a shadowy recollection of sitting on somebody's knee, and know-ing that it was his father), that is about all that is knowable. A photograph of him shows a handsome young man, brimming with plausibility and charm. His father had died when he was sixteen; his mother disapproved his leaving Clemson, and disapproved his courtship of my grandmother, who was not only from Virginia, but an Episcopalian (and in Horry County that wasn't much dif-ferent from being a papist or an out and out heathen) to boot. But

she could not change her son's mind and relented to the extent of deeding him a parcel of land across the road from Snow Hill, where still a bachelor, he built the fine Queen Anne house my parents now live in. Real Frances was embarrassed by her fiancé's confidence; engagements were as risky as pregnancies, and she refused to jeopardize hers by entering the house, or even looking at it, until she and Arthur were safely and irrevocably married.

He banked on hope and the fortune he intended to make. There were losses even before he lost his arm, and growing debt. But when disaster came, and left him looking more like a war veteran than his father ever did, he seems to have been without self-pity or bitterness. Lucille would tell me how, after the amputation, he liked to have her tie his necktie for him, because, as he teased her, she was the only person hard-hearted enough to do it without crying. The two trains he made for his sons still exist—they are handsome, heavy things, and do not look toys, but like real locomotives, inferring, on a smaller scale, power, mass, and purpose.

Daddy learned to walk more or less inadvertently by pushing his along its track. Both are beautifully built; the parts look interchangeable, and you cannot tell that one of them was made by a man working with one hand, and that the wrong hand.

Debt mounted; the sawmill began losing money, and he took a job that a one-armed man, or any man at all, could do: night superintendent in a plant downriver, at a place called Pitch Landing. The plant, "Southern Wood Products," struck him as unsafe, but he could not afford safety. Its boiler exploded on the night of 14 August 1912; he was a week shy of his thirty-first birthday.

As the widow of a man whose future had been foreclosed, Real Frances could not hold on to the house he had built for her. It was sold at public auction. She and her sons lived briefly with her mother-in-law, then, also briefly, with her own parents, until she was able to buy a small house on Main Street. Here my father and his brother grew up. As a boy, Daddy could see from his window trains coming down Main street, pulling flatcars piled high with logs from the Pee Dee basin. Or sometimes not piled at all— sometimes a single pine log, its diameter at the butt more than man-high. Logging camps were soon established wherever there was timber; one was called Forney, after the locomotive that had once run on the elevated railways of Manhattan, and there is still a community of that name out on Highway 378, in handsome farm country just east of where the road crosses the Pee Dee at Potato Bed Ferry. Within two decades of Arthur's death, the sturdy little engines had brought past Real Frances's door the last of a great forest, one that we can scarcely remember. It had been the kingdom of the ivory-billed woodpecker and the Carolina parakeet and the panther and, for all we know, of fauns and dryads.

Real Frances kept the books at Stilley Plywood; she took in boarders, lived austerely, and raised her sons. The First World War came, and all our century's woe began; the boys took turns being gallant Yank and perifidious Hun in the backyard. The first-growth forest went fast; my father would never see it. But he

129

could walk out from his doorstep with dog and gun, cross Main Street, go about half a block north, and find the first covey in what is now the Episcopal Church parking lot. It had been the descendants of these birds, more steadfast than most human memory, that I would sometimes see scurrying down Applewhite Lane when I was on my way to Lucille's. They lived in hedges between yards, and in the tangled ditchbank beside the church.

Addie Burroughs died in 1918 and left not much but something to her son's widow. Finally, in 1928, with both her sons about to finish college, Real Frances re-acquired the house Arthur had built for her. As it would be for my parents when they moved back to it, it was really more of a house than she needed, but there was obviously a great steadfastness in her, too.

I don't know whether she ever recalled her initial misgivings about the confidence with which her husband-to-be had built the house, letting his imagination run ahead of his circumstances. It was to have been full of children, like Snow Hill; instead it became the place she inhabited alone, although visited pretty frequently by her grandchildren. By the time I came to consciousness, both she and the house seemed indigenous to this spot, as unremovable from it as the big sycamore that grew in the front yard. As far as I know, she kept her thoughts very much to herself. She lived to see one of her two sons, my uncle Jack, and one of her three grandchildren, my sister Coles, buried in the plot beside Arthur. I remember standing beside her in church, hearing her read out the responses in a voice that still had a good deal of Virginia in it, and thinking that the English of *The Book of Common Prayer* had been her first language, and that she still probably had her quietest, most private thoughts in its austerely consoling phrases.

After Addie died, Snow Hill passed into the hands of Donald, her youngest son. In 1921, he decided to renovate. I have never understood exactly what he planned to do, but it involved adding some massive brick columns to the front of the old house, to give it a kind of swagger. It also and simultaneously involved a new paint job. Somebody decided that the best way to remove the old paint from pine clapboards, baked dry by the sun and full of resin, would be with a blow torch.

When the rubble had cooled, Donald built himself a pleasant, handsome house, vaguely Mediterranean in style. The grounds accepted it gracefully—a big magnolia grew close to its west end; ivy covered its walls, and it came to look, to me and my generation of cousins, as though it had always been there. Donald was a tidy man, but for some reason he did not bother to destroy the brick columns that had been part of his renovation scheme, and that of course survived the fire. Perhaps they served to remind him of the dangers of thinking too big. Ivy grew up over them too, and they looked like the relics of something ancient. If they had been in England, you would have supposed them the remains of an abbey or monastery vandalized by Henry VIII. A different kind of supposition attaches to them in South Carolina. Each spring, there are loosely organized tours of Conway; Canadians, down for the golf and sunshine at Myrtle Beach, seem particularly drawn to them. A few years ago, a group of such tourists was passing through, and I saw a woman point out the columns to her husband. He was a fine, brisk-looking man, with a precise mustache. He solemnly regarded the columns for a moment, then shook his head in curt acknowledgment of historical calamity. "Sherman," he said.

Which brings us back to the porch, where Mama, Daddy, and I sat on this still, heavy day in March. Renovation and expansion were again in progress at Snow Hill. It seemed to be going better this time. Donald's house now belonged to one of his grandnieces and her husband, and they had fully doubled its size. In this latest avatar, the house at Snow Hill had no pretensions to modesty. From the water, it had looked huge, more like something belonging to the Loire Valley than the Kingston Lake swamps. Its symmetrical and calculated grandeur seemed to assert a new style of

Southern oligarchy here, one that acknowledged no financial, psychological, or architectural kinship to the county. But there was an old local precedent for a residence on this scale and of this opulence. It lay in the mirage that Plowden Weston and his class had left behind them, even here, in a town that had looked like the last place God made.

# 5   Conway to Sandy Island

I hung around Conway for three pleasant days, waiting on the weekend. Ricky McIver and I had arranged to take this last part of the trip together. He had to work until midday Saturday, but could get the following Monday off. We used Saturday afternoon to round up gear and food, and to take my truck down to Georgetown and leave it there. We embarked at a gentlemanly hour on Sunday morning.

After considerable discussion about it, we had decided to take one of his canoes, rather than continuing in mine. There would be big wakes to contend with in the lower river, and his had a higher bow. It also had a shallow semi-vee bottom, which serious canoeists—and Ricky is nothing if not a serious canoeist—pronounce to be faster than the traditional rounded bottom. Offsetting these advantages was the fact that his canoe was made of fiberglass, and had all the aesthetic interest of a laundromat. But I had, on the one hand, had four days in which to contemplate the ribbed and varnished beauty of my own canoe, and on the other hand, forty years in which to contemplate the adamantine obduracy of Ricky McIver's convictions, so I yielded the point.

The weather had warmed up. The oaks were in the rich fullness of early leaf, wisteria hung in purple and thickly perfumed clusters all over Conway. Behind us, in the yard at Snow Hill, such azaleas as had survived a murderous February freeze were coming into blossom. We slipped down the Lake, under the bridge, past the Presbyterian Church, and entered the Waccamaw.

Ricky's canoe had felt tippy and skittish as we loaded the gear and got into it, but it seemed to gain stability as it gained momentum, like a bicycle. We kept a steady pace, using shorter paddles and a quicker rhythm than I was accustomed to. When we pushed ourselves, the stern rose slightly, as though the canoe were riding on its own wake. We needed to cover twenty-five miles today, and would have the tide against us until noon. For the first five miles, one or the other of us would silently increase the tempo, half as a challenge, half as an experiment, and we would boil along for a hundred yards or so. Then the softness of the day, or a wood-duck preening on a log, or a fine clump of cherokee roses hanging out over the river would give us an excuse to slow back down, and we'd loiter and dawdle. It was like tuning one of the old outboard motors we used to fool with—adjusting the spark and throttle, trying to coax a few more rpm from the engine, and instead sending it into a fit of coughing and sputtering. But by the time we got to Pitch Landing, where Grandaddy had come to grief, we were in synch and balanced off against each other, making time.

By mid-morning, we were to Pott Bluff, as far up as schooners normally came. You could see why they stopped here. Just above Pott Bluff there was an oxbow, the first one that a vessel coming upstream would have encountered, and it made an unusually convoluted loop off to the east. A thoroughfare of about a mile in length had been cut early in the nineteenth century, and the state periodically allocated small sums to maintaining it, but it was apparently not a satisfactory ship-channel. And so, until the advent of the steamboat and the railroad in the final decades of the nineteenth century, Pott Bluff remained the usual entrepot for anything being shipped into central Horry, and was to Conway what Ostia was to Rome. We had now seen the last of the sandbars and sandy levees so characteristic of the upper river, and dry land of any sort would be in increasingly short supply. The swamps here are always wet, even in summer.

Geologically, the country grows newer as you descend the river; historically, it is older—older at least in terms of the history that gets recorded in documents and written on landscapes by people determined to insulate themselves from the ebb and flow of natural events. We were still above the ricefield country. Most of the enterprise along this section of the river had been associated with the Buck family, who had come into lower Horry in 1830. The Bucks had a predilection for big rivers, and made their fortunes and left their names beside them, first along the mighty Penobscot in Maine, where, having moved up from Boston prior to the Revolution, they founded Bucksport, sawed white pine, and built ships for three generations. One of the third generation, Henry, then lit out for the southern frontier and fetched up on the banks of the Waccamaw. He came far enough up the river to be out of the domain of the rice planters, where land was expensive and the swamps were already cleared, and then settled down to pursue the family vocation, sawing the virgin oak and yellow pine from the Waccamaw basin. Within twenty years of his arrival, he had joined the planter aristocracy of the lower river, and purchased Woodbourne plantation, but Horry lumber remained the basis of his wealth.

Henry Buck lost no opportunity to propagate the family name; between Pott Bluff and Bull Creek, Ricky and I would paddle past Buck's Upper Mill, Bucksville, and Buck's Lower Mill, as it was known in the nineteenth century, although it is now called Bucksport. The Northern and Southern branches of the family kept in close communication. The Maine woods had been ransacked; as early as 1846, Thoreau found that the big pines were gone. Henry

Buck's operation kept the yards along the Penobscot humming; the forests of the Waccamaw emigrated north, in Yankee ships, to build more Yankee ships. One of these, the bark *Henry Buck,* 594 tons, was named in honor of the Carolina branch of the family; she set sail in 1852. But most pleasing to me—commerce reenacting the myth of Alpheus and Arethusa, one river passing beneath the sea to rise, in a new form, in a distant land—was the brig *Waccamaw,* which slid down the ways into the Penobscot in 1855. Perhaps she gave her home port simply as Bucksport, so both states could claim her. She passed beneath the sea, to rise no more, in 1865, just when the Civil War's long interruption of her regular trade—Penobscot ice for Waccamaw lumber—was at last over.

But the war did not break the Buck family. On its eve, Gilmore found old Mr. Henry Buck a staunch Unionist, a slave-owner who had none of the usual paternalistic delusions about the loyalty and devotion of his slaves. His two sons nevertheless unimpeachably served the new and short-lived country of which they suddenly found themselves citizens. While the mills stood silent along the Waccamaw, they carried on a different kind of commerce with Yankeedom, one dying on John's Island, near Charleston, and the other being captured in 1864 at Petersburg, in the last, brutal slogging of the Virginia campaign. Once the war was over, there were no hard feelings, and the Bucks of Maine and South Carolina went back to business. By 1867, Henry Buck, of Bucksville, South Carolina, had a third interest in the bark *Hudson,* built that year in Bucksport, Maine. And a few years after that, a contingent of shipwrights from the Penobscot moved down to the Waccamaw and established a boatyard at Bucksville.

In retrospect, there is a sadness to it, although it could not have seemed so to this enterprising family, who had for so many years, through the upheaval of Revolution and Civil War, gone on building wooden ships, and who, having found a new and seemingly inexhaustible supply of timber in this underdeveloped Southern backwater, must have dreamed of an actual city rising here, a counterpart to the northern Bucksport, a place with brick buildings and sidewalks and a life of its own, with commerce, art, and civilization. Not very long after I moved to Maine, I went to visit its Bucksport, and found it a handsome, dignified town, no longer particularly busy, except for a paper plant at the north end, but full of fine nineteenth-century houses and commercial buildings. It had successfully translated an evanescent prosperity into something solid, substantial, and lasting, and has the staid, matronly air of an old seaport town.

Bucksville would not be thus. Wooden ships, although reaching unprecedented size and speed in the last half of the nineteenth century, would build no more cities along the Atlantic seaboard. The schooner *Hattie McGilvery Buck*, perhaps a pilot project, was built at Bucksville in 1874, and this experiment was apparently successful enough to warrant a larger one. This was the *Henrietta*—probably named for some beloved wife or sister, but it is tempting to think that Henry Buck had simply sent his name out upon the waters again, this time in a feminine declension. She was a clipper ship of 1,267 tons. By now there were between sixty and a hundred relocated Maine shipwrights in Bucksville, and one of them, S. S. Stevens, executed a couple of watercolors of the shipyard, with the *Henrietta* under construction. These are now in the Penobscot Marine Museum.

In Stevens' paintings, the *Henrietta* lies on the shore, at the edge of the river. Her hull is largely complete, although still surrounded by scaffolding—perhaps caulking or painting is in progress. The masts and rigging are not yet in place. The hull completely overwhelms Bucksville—it is as though an ordinary sized rowboat had been pulled into the pretend village of a child's sandbox. Because the artist was not skilled, there is no doubt distortion of scale and perspective. But I expect that his amateurish effort is true to the emotional, if not the visual, effect of the *Henrietta*. Compared to its massive grace, the slipshod community behind it would have

137

seemed like little more than the casual debris that surrounds any construction project. During the time that it was being built, the clipper would have loomed over Bucksville like a cathedral over the huts and houses of a medieval town, and would have been comparably portentous.

Both North and South, the story goes that the *Henrietta* cost $90,000 to build. A comparable ship built in Maine at the same time cost $115,000. But there is disagreement as to why Bucksville did not, on the basis of this, go on to build more ships and become the queen city of the lower Waccamaw, the cynosure of all Horry. The Northern version of the story is that the *Henrietta*, big as she was, was not big enough—a few years after her launching, there slid down the ways of a shipyard in Bath, Maine, a clipper of twice her tonnage, setting a new standard in the twilit magnificence of the age of sail. A vessel of such proportions could never have made it from Bucksville, down the Waccamaw, and out across the bar in Winyah Bay. Further, the Yankee chronicler of the Buck family points out, very reasonably, that shipbuilding was becoming increasingly an operation involving specialists-"caulkers, joiners, sparmakers, blacksmiths, etc."—to whom much of the work was subcontracted. In a major shipbuilding city like Bath or Bucksport, Maine, these specialties had evolved into independent businesses, and they could count on the shipyards, and the shipyards could count on them. Bucksville, still a frontier village, lacked an infrastructure. To these reasons for Bucksville's failure to become a major spawning ground for Yankee clippers, we may plausibly add that Maine shipwrights must have found it hard duty down in the malarial swamps, beneath the savage summer sun, and could be forgiven for abandoning this brave new colony of Buckdom for the hygienically cold comforts of New England.

But the Southern custodian of the Buck legacy—Mrs. Eugenia Cutts, mother of Ricky's and my crony and classmate, Henry Buck Cutts (always called Buck and never, except by such obtuse agencies as the Selective Service System or the Internal Revenue Service, Henry)— speculates along different lines. She conjectures that the Yankee cousins saw that their experiment would, if allowed to continue, drive them off the market. They had plenty of leverage, since they were the primary purchasers of lumber from the upper, middle, and lower mills, and so they quietly squelched the incipient rival they had created. Horry Buckdom remained a colony of Downeast Buckdom, a supplier of raw resources and a purchaser of finished goods. The Revolution and Civil War were in part occasioned by this sort of arrangement, but, as far as I know, relations between the two branches of the family remained close and cordial, and even now most of the Waccamaw River clan sooner or later make the pilgrimage up to the Penobscot, and gaze at Stevens' painting of the *Henrietta*, and acquaint themselves with the latest generation of their cousins.

The *Henrietta* lasted less than twenty years. In 1894, having taken on eight hundred tons of manganese ore and crockery at Yokahama, she proceeded to Kobe to pick up the rest of a cargo bound for New York. A typhoon caught her at the harbor mouth and drove her ashore. The cargo was salvaged but the ship was irreparable. And so it came to pass that, in a thrifty, unforested country a world away from the swamps that grew it, the fine oak and pine timber of the *Henrietta* was hacked and sawed and splintered for a last time, and sold in small bunches as kindling, and the first and final Waccamaw clipper went up in smoke.

Some years and generations later, circa 1955, my father purchased from Henry Lee Buck III, Eugenia Cutts's brother, a flatbottomed cypress paddling boat approximately twelve feet long, thirty inches amidships, and displacing .05 tons, soaking wet. We christened it the *H. L. Buck* and kept it moored to a cypress tree at Little Savannah. It disappeared from its mooring in 1959; thereafter, vague reports circulated of its having been seen, repainted, tethered to a piling at Red Bluff or stashed under the eaves of a tobacco barn at Wampee or Tilly Swamp. But we never tracked it down, and soon even rumors of its existence ceased, and the last nominal heir of the *Henry Buck*, the *Alice Buck*, the *Fanny Buck*, the *Hattie McGilvery Buck*, and the *Henrietta* must be presumed extinct.

The Buck sawmills continued to cut lumber, and the river was busy with shipping. As late as 1890, 6 million board feet of pine and cypress were cut at Bucksville, and 4 million cypress shingles were made there. An article in *The Charleston World* for 1891 describes it as a thriving place, where land remains miraculously inexpensive and pestilence is no problem, thanks to the proximity of Cowford Springs, "a mineral water which has become famous because of its wonderful medicinal qualities." The article is illustrated with pen and ink drawings, showing the church, an inn, a masonic lodge, and the waterfront, with a schooner, *The City of Baltimore*, tied up at the docks. Behind *The City of Baltimore* the massive brick chimney of the sawmill rises above the trees. At its zenith, Bucksville had seven hundred citizens, three churches, two hotels, and "several private schools," which must have given it more private schools per capita than even Cambridge, Massachusetts.

But the city did not take, as Conway, a smaller town further upriver, did. It remained an adventitiuos encampment, dependent, like any boom town, on a diminishing natural resource. The article in *The Charleston World* was obviously intended as a promotional booster, but it seems not to have fooled anybody. By the turn of the century, Bucksport—the lower mill—had eclipsed Bucksville, probably because it had readier access to the Pee Dee basin and the timber there. In 1904 the Bucksville mill burned, and the town seems to have evaporated instantly. Now, as Ricky and I paddled past, there remained the one abiding landmark, familiar to us for as long as we had known this part of the river, and as unchanging and unquestioned as an articulation of local geology. The brick chimney of the mill that devoured so much of the Waccamaw forest now rises out of a tangle of honeysuckle and catbriar, and barely keeps its head above the thicket at its

base. Nothing around it explains it—there is no trace of the docks that were here, or of the "four immense longitudinal boilers" which, according to the *World*, "ran two monster engines aggregating several hundred horsepower" which in turn drove great gang saws, lathes, trimmers, edgers, planers, butt saws and rip saws, all "of modern pattern, capable of turning out the maximum results." There are extinct towns in New England too, and you know them by the stone cellar holes and stone fences that remain, the apple trees that still live in the understory of the woods, and the lilacs that hang on, close by what had been the dooryard. But Bucksville is simply gone—a town that boasted doctors and lawyers, bankers and even a dentist.

There is an unimproved landing just below the chimney, and inland from it the usual pattern of fields and thick woods, with the usual scattering of farmhouses. Nothing distinguishes this place from any other rural place in Horry County. To me it was notable because, when I used to come to it early in the morning, to fish the good stretch of river just upstream, there was normally a great horned owl in the vicinity of the old chimney, and, as I dragged the boat down to launch it out on dark water that still reflected the stars, he would hoot, booming, portentous, and peremptory, and fill me with some obscure sense of trespass. Once or twice, coming back at dusk, I saw him, gliding, as owls always do, below the tree line, a big bird to be sure, but far smaller than the rumors of himself that he disseminated in the early morning darkness.

A haunted quality thickens as you descend the Waccamaw. You begin to encounter a past that now seems as remote as the one that was wept for by the waters of Babylon. Hard to believe now how prosaic it all once was, how mundane to the people for whom it was simply a fact of their time, the way that the highway bridges and the glittering sprawl of developed beachland a few miles to our east were facts of our time. Bishop in all probability saw the *Hattie McGilvery Buck* or the *Henrietta* under construction; he certainly saw the clouds of steam and plums of smoke rising from the sawmills, and the docks piled high with lumber and naval stores. Certainly he must have seen proud schooners being loaded, and perhaps encountered one, pulled by a sturdy steam-tug, its big propellor churning and splashing, coming up against the tide from Georgetown. But he mentions none of this; it all no doubt seemed to him too familiar for words.

On the east bank of the river, with scant exception, there was no dry land, only long, wide miles of swamp. As the river widens, it loses its intimacy. The swamps form a looming, solid wall, broken only by the occasional creek that soon loses itself in the deep shadows. As the tide turned, late in the morning, we could not only feel but even hear the change, as the water, held back by the high tide, now began a sighing retreat from the swamp. It was

142

as though, far downstream, a plug had been pulled, and the waters were being withdrawn by a huge suction.

We had passed the chimney at Bucksville a little before the noon whistle would have blown, if there had been steam to blow it and mills hands to hear it. Two miles further down was Peachtree Landing, about the only place between Conway and Georgetown County where high land, which is to say dry land, comes down to the east side of the river. We decided to stop here for lunch. The landing sits on a channel that loops away from the main river, and Ricky and I had occasionally come here to camp, during our high school years. Daddy could remember a ferry here, but it had probably never been particularly busy. Between Peachtree and the Atlantic there hadn't been much but savannah and sand-dune, land that had supported only a few meagre farms. Now, after three decades of accelerating speculation and development, this same land was mostly motel, golf course, condominium, retirement community, restaurant, and mini-mall, but so far these things had not reached the river itself. We pulled out beneath a big pine and strolled around a bit. Just away from the river were some shallow excavations in a vein of yellow clay, which suggested that there might have once been a small brick kiln here, and we could see, in a grove of young pines, the pattern of old furrows. It was pleasant to take a break from paddling. The young pines were full of yellow jessamine, and its perfume mixed sweetly through the heavy, almost soporific aroma of sun-warmed pine needles.

We came back to the big pine beside the water, sat with our backs to it, and ate lunch. While we had been walking, a few white clouds had begun massing themselves, and now we watched them building up into thunderheads. There was a premonitory growling of thunder, and with the sky still blue above us, a hard spattering of rain. The first drops were so widely spaced that they pelted and stung without wetting us; each made a distinct crater in the dust. But the pace picked up rapidly, and what had sounded like the hesitant tapping of an untrained typist began to assume rhythm and cadence, and the rain came in drum rolls. The river, pocked and slashed, shone jagged and silver in front of us, an expanse of punctured tin. It seemed the rain could come no harder, but it came harder, and the far bank of the river disappeared in a smoky haze. We hunkered in the lee of the pine; there was a gust of suddenly refrigerated air, and the raindrops grew animate, bounced and rolled like water spilled onto a hot stove. Hail, then. We hung onto our hats. "Better now than when the crops are up," I yelled to Ricky over the storm; "Better on some goddamn golfer's head than mine," he yelled back, but I could hear the exuberance in it, his elation at this small, sharp display of natural violence. The hailstones were not quite the size of popcorn, which they resembled in the way they burst into being at our feet. The sun was gone; a few branches and cones, shaken from the pine, fell into the river in front of us, joining other minor arboreal jetsam, bobbing and pitching like wreckage in the black water. Our pine was the tallest thing around, and therefore the least safe place to shelter; both of us knew that, and neither of us suggested moving. Two peals of thunder were close, with that sky-shattering quality that was, for so much of human history, the most terrible noise imaginable to man. We saw one lightning bolt—a flash of neon across the river, momentarily revealing to us, through a dusky, shivering atmosphere, the pitching and swaying of the swamp trees.

And then it ended, as though it had been an hallucination, a *delirium tremens* of the macrocosm. A wonderful, oxygen-charged aftercoolness hung in the air briefly; here beside this low country river there was the distinct feeling of standing beside a waterfall, in an alpine, balsam-scented country. That passed before the hail melted on the ground, where it already looked odd and out of place, like styrofoam pellets spilled from a passing truck. We unloaded the canoe and dumped a few pints of gin-clear sky water into the black Waccamaw. By the time we had reloaded and resumed paddling the sun was out. My shirt quickly dried across my shoulders, and felt warm and light, as though freshly laundered and ironed.

The air was brighter and brisker in the wake of the storm. Ricky took the stern, and we settled back into the rhythm of paddling. Below Peachtree, we entered an unfamiliar stretch of river, but it offered nothing new to our inspection. The banks were low and swampy, with an occasional hummock. A big outboard skiff, flat-bottomed and locally made, passed us, headed upriver. It looked like a shad fisherman, and shortly after he went by, we came upon what must have been his camp, a rather elaborate shelter made of lashed saplings and covered with plastic sheeting; empty clorox bottles were scattered around, along with rope, canned goods, and what Huck Finn would have called his traps—the miscellaneous pots, clothing, and whatnot that you lug around through life. It cheered us both to see a campsite so entirely uninfluenced by L. L. Bean. Clorox bottles have been used as floats by shad fishermen for at least thirty years, to my certain knowledge. They used to be made of glass, with a looped handle on the neck that made it easy to attach them to the net. Nowadays they are plastic, and, while still perfectly adequate, have no particular advantage over plastic milk jugs, plastic anti-freeze bottles, or dozens of other containers. But it was pleasing to see that this shad fisherman was a traditionalist, loyal to the old brand. His camp was on the right-hand bank, pleasantly situated on a point formed between the river and what appeared to be an oxbow lake. Oddly enough, there was another oxbow lake on the opposite side of the river, creating a long, narrow pond.

We paddled across the pond, talking about shad fishing. It was in Horry County very much a farmer's recreation; Ricky thought that this was probably because shad season coincided with a slack time of the agricultural year, and offered a last opportunity for a man so disposed to get away for a week, live beside the river, do some uncensored drinking, and, if he was lucky, have shad to sell when he came back home to face the ploughing, and the foregone futility of his summer's toil: the bedding and the transplanting, suckering, poisoning, and weeding of the tobacco, and then the back-breaking harvest, leaf by leaf, as August began; then the tying, curing, packing, and selling.

In general, shad fishermen had the reputation of being a rough lot, and Ricky recounted for me a camping trip that he and our mutual cousin Sam Dargan had taken, something more than a quarter of a century before. They had gone down to Peachtree on a rainy Friday in March, and found it occupied by a pair of shad fishermen. The river was high, it was getting dark, and there was no other place to camp, so the fishermen told Ricky and Sam to pull up and share the spot with them. They accepted, although with some misgivings—the campsite was strewn with bottles, empty cans, skeletal remains of fish, and so much other debris that Ricky wondered if some of it hadn't been brought along for purely orna- mental purposes, to make the place feel homey. A campfire burned on the remains of an old truck tire; several more tires were stashed under a tarp, for future use.

Ricky and Sam were at this time conscientious members of the Boy Scouts of America, and had come prepared to build an ele- gant tepee of twigs over a pile of laboriously whittled shavings, to make the sort of tidy campfire the Scout's Handbook man- dated, and then to unfold their aluminium mess-kits, and boil up something virtuous, like oatmeal sprinkled with raisins and nuts. They fumbled around with the wet wood, shivering in the rain, struck matches and watched their fire fizzle out. The fishermen observed, in a silent, objective way—not pretending not to notice or to have anything better to do, and not feeling called upon to offer advice, encouragement, or any other form of acknowledge- ment. Ricky said it was like being studied by two unusually sombre owls. Finally one of them spoke, and said they might as well use a fire that was burning already, so Ricky and Sam moved over to the smouldering tire and cooked their oatmeal. It didn't taste very good or digest very well, but they ate it, conscious now of the scrutiny not only of the two fishermen, but of a great, disapproving Scoutmaster in the sky.

Eventually, with a pity akin to that which the Massachusetts Indians felt for the hapless pilgrims, the men offered Ricky and Sam a deal, and said they'd look after the cooking if the boys would look after the cleaning up, and so, for the rest of the weekend, that was what they did. At mealtime, one of the fishermen would take a tire, set it in the ashes, souse it with gasoline, stand back a ways, and toss it a match. There would be a *whoosh* that shook the earth, and flame and black smoke would swirl and billow to the treetops. When the fire had subsided enough to permit him to get in range, the cook would put on an iron frying pan with some lard in it, open a couple of cans, and dump the contents into the pan. All the labels had been washed off by the rain; it was impossible to tell what was going into the pan and impossible to tell what came out of it—simply a blackened mass of generic food. After the first meal, Ricky set to scouring the pan with sand and water, the recommended Boy Scout procedure. The two men again watched long enough to satisfy their ethnological curiosity, then one of them came over, took the pan, and threw it out into the night. The idea seemed to be that rain, sun, and raccoons should do the preliminary cleaning—if you washed a pot too far in advance of its next use, it would only get dirty in the interval. So Ricky learned to wash the pan and plates (which followed the pan into outer darkness) just at meal time, while the tire was being kindled. The pan itself, black, crusted, and warped by heat, resembled a souvenir from fairly close to ground zero, he said.

As we talked and laughed about this story, I was half conscious that, after we had crossed the narrow pond formed by the double oxbow, the river bent to the right, forming a serpentine curve as sharp as any on the upper Waccamaw. But we were making good time, and after the long straight stretches, this bend was welcome, with the small promise and suspense that every river bend holds as to what lies beyond it. And this time there was a surprise sure enough. We rounded the bend on the inside and there, pleasantly situated on a point, was a rather elaborate shelter made of lashed saplings and covered with plastic sheeting, empty clorox bottles were scattered around, etc.

I stopped paddling and was very glad that this had not happened to me when I was travelling alone. Let Ricky explain it. Ricky said nothing. I could only think that the last time we had seen this place, it had been on the right-hand side of the river. Now it was on the left. It was as though you were to read on the back of this page what you had just got through reading on the front of it. Would Ricky now start his story again from the beginning, about how he and Sam Dargan had gone down to Peachtree on a rainy Friday in March, something more than a quarter of a century ago?

Instead he laughed. "Either I'm having a fairly acute attack of *déjà vu*, or we've just gone in a circle. That was an island in the river, and we went right around it. The river goes that way." He pointed to the left, which did seem to be the only unexplored possibility, and was, of course, the right one. Just below the fisherman's camp, the Waccamaw zigged sharply to the east, before zagging back again to its southerly course. Back in Conway, I told this story to my cousin Henry, who had begun his career in the lumber business back when the Waccamaw steamers were still in service. He laughed, but said that we weren't the first to make a round trip at the Needle's Eye, and at least we hadn't had passengers on board, silently betting on whether or not we'd take the wrong turn.

Just above Bucksport, né Buck's Lower Mill, the Intracoastal Waterway Canal comes into the Waccamaw, and the river grows yet larger. A canoe or small boat begins to feel precarious and presumptuous out in the middle of it, and we kept close in along the bank. There is a wharf along the waterfront at Bucksport; at low tide, you can see among its pilings stones that came down as ballast on New England ships. A well-equipped marina and a restaurant of good reputation are here now, to take advantage of the yachting trade. A sleek forty-footer was tied up at the wharf today, all glass and glittering chrome. A woman lay in a recliner on the rear deck. She was reading a newspaper. She glanced down at us, then quickly back to the newspaper, as though she feared that we might ask for a handout. Even the engines of the yacht sounded rich—a low, throaty burbling astern, swilling into the spring air a heady bouquet of diesel exhaust.

Back in behind Bucksport lies savannah land, black, gummy soil that drains poorly, and a sizeable portion of it was given by the Buck family to their slaves after the Civil War. No doubt many of these stayed in the vicinity to work in the shingle mill and sawmills that continued to operate at Bucksport well into the twentieth century, but this impromptu community, unlike the more elaborate one at Bucksville, has outlasted the mills. There was never a village, only a patchwork of tiny farms, many with fields scarcely larger than garden plots. The men and women who have stayed on here had to go to Conway or Georgetown or Myrtle Beach to find work, and that was generally no more than menial work: housemaids or yardmen in Conway; chambermaids and maintenance men at Myrtle Beach.

I had some sense that this was a special sort of place. In Conway, the black community at Bucksport had a good name; its people were considered to be hard workers, reliable, honest, civil, and so forth. Their speech set them apart. It may have had some element of Gullah in it; my ear is not educated enough to be certain. But its rhythms were distinct from any other black or white speech of Horry County: quicker, more staccato, and somehow implosive, as though the words were not being projected from the mouth out into the air so much as they were being snapped out of the air and spoken inwardly, almost swallowed.

On their own ground, they were not people to be trifled with. As a summer employee of the United States Agricultural Stabilization Corporation, I had once spent a broiling July afternoon looking for one particular Bucksport farmer, so that I might measure his tobacco patch to be sure that he had not overplanted. I would knock at a door, and ask after Mr. Fred so-and-so; I got no curses or scowls, or even what you would positively call unfriendliness. I met many people who didn't believe they knew a Mr. *Fred* so-and-so; was I sure it warn't *Roscoe* so-and-so? So I would be directed to Roscoe's, and Roscoe would not be home, and his wife would say he didn't plant tobacco nohow and send me off to somebody else who *might* know Fred, and that person would not only not know Fred, but would profess never to have even heard of Roscoe, much less Roscoe's wife.

I was sixteen years old, ignorant as dirt, and certain that the United States Department of Agriculture, disguised as the sun that pounded down on the tin-roofed houses and the brick-hard earth, was watching my every move, timing me. The sun dropped slowly, and the dashboard clock ticked an imperturbable counterpoint to my impatience, then urgency, then panic, as though it were scheduled to detonate an explosive device at precisely five o'clock, at which time, in theory, I should be back at the ASC office in Conway, having measured and cut down to size not only Mr. Fred so-and-so's field, but also two others, over by Klondike. But instead of measuring tobacco, I was standing, hat in hand, a suppliant, on porches or outside of doors, on lawns that had no grass, no shade trees, no escape from the sun.

It did not occur to me that, in a matter of only a few decades, it would all seem terribly funny, this incipient and frustrated little bureaucrat bouncing back and forth across roads of baked mud, receiving contradictory delphic instructions from beyond the uncrossable thresholds of race, class, education, and experience. The country was featureless, the houses distinguishable to me in my agitation only by the make of automobile parked beside them.

The roads formed a regular grid, as though for a city that hadn't happened. Finally, late in the day—far too late for me to get back to Conway before five o'clock—a trick occurred to me. People were now coming home from their jobs in town, and I waved one battered station wagon down.

It was full of men and women, none of whom looked anymore communicative than the ones I'd been talking to all afternoon. I leaned out of the window of the green USDA truck I was in, and tried to sound official. "I got a package here for a Mr." I said, and pretended to look down at the seat beside me, "a Mr. Fred so-and-so. At least I think that's what it says. Anybody like that live around here?" And it worked; one of them said "Dar he, settin' on 'iz poach," and pointed back to a house I had just come from and a man I'd just talked to.

So I went up to his porch, sweaty, flustered, and too conscious of being a fool even to feel entitled to anger. "You're Mr. Fred so-and-so?" I asked him "Dazz RITE!" He said it as though I'd just given a correct answer on a quiz show. "Well I'm here to measure your tobacco." He gave me a quick look, with a glint of slyness: "Way you drivin' 'round to ever body house, seem like you from the CENSUS bureau. But I tell you abow 'at tobacco. I get me contrak and plant'em', get'em sot out good, and come a big rain. 'At tobacco drownt, all but two-tree row. Taint enough to bodder 'bout; taint enough in 'at field to chaw." Then he took me behind the house and showed me. The field was grown over with weeds; a few tobacco plants were visible, scattered here and there. "Hep youself," he said, all hospitality. He was right—it wasn't enough to bother about. I went to the office next morning expecting to get chewed out. The supervisor questioned me, took a few notes, and told me to do the Klondike farms that morning. I never heard anything else about it, but at the end of the week found I was paid for an hour and fifteen minutes of overtime.

It was past three o'clock when we left Bucksport astern. Neither of us was very clear on how far it was to Bull Creek, where we planned to camp. So we put our backs into it, although the afternoon only grew softer and more languid as it declined. The swamps below Bucksport were full of cherokee rose and wild azalea, and the yellow jessamine was draped like Christmas tinsel over the lower branches of streamside trees. We now first began to see, flitting elusively at the swamp edge, prothonotary warblers. I had expected to find them all along the river; I remembered them as being almost its most characteristic bird. But apparently it was still too early for them to have reached the upper Waccamaw. In the sombre understory of the swamps where they live, they are implausibly brilliant, like something that ought to inhabit a coral reef or a rain-forest. Other warblers are bright, but these seem incandescent. When you look at one in the deep shade, against the black water, perched for one vivid instant, nuthatch-like, on a cypress knee, the bird is so luminous that its image is slightly blurred, like that of a candle flame. Then with a flick of its tail it is gone, although seldom far; most of its flights are power-assisted hops, from branch to twig to rotting leaf-mold, busy as a chickadee, although without the same plump and cheerful assurance. Its eyes are remarkably black, a small bead of ink, as surprising to find in the bird's golden plumage as the bird itself is in the darkness of the swamp.

A mile below Bucksport we met a big yacht coming upriver. We had been warned of such things, but there was little enough we could do about it; it was going to be a pretty stiff problem. The widening furrow of its wake looked to be four or five feet, from trough to peak, and these swells were steep, cresting as they came. The effect was positively unreal: the sleek and sky-mirroring river, smooth as milk, the steady, muffled throbbing of the yacht's diesels, and an actual surf curling itself up into rolling cylinders that began at the bow wave of the yacht and ended with the slamming collapse of water along the swampy shore. Ricky kept us well out in the river, where there was no danger of being caught in the breaking of the wake, but where the interval between swells was shorter and steeper. We climbed the first one, taking it slightly on the quarter, plunged down its back, and burrowed the bow into the next one, scooping up a gallon or so of river before we reached the crest, slid over, and into the diminishing waves that followed. After we had wallowed our way back to equilibrium, we turned to watch the yacht. It forged steadily on; the helmsman never looked back, and something in the rigidity of this posture made me wonder if he had not hardened himself against the echoing oaths that followed him from Miami to Manhattan. The Waccamaw surged and rolled itself out smooth again; we took consolation in reflections of a village-bolshevist sort, and continued on our way.

To reduce our exposure to yacht traffic, we turned into Silvers Creek, which loops away from the river and then rejoins it a mile downstream. It was a narrow, enclosed place, the trees almost shutting out the sky. The prothonotary warblers were close beside us here, escorting us it seemed, or darting across the stream. Their complete silence seemed pointed; one expected so bright a bird to have something to say for itself. Halfway along the creek we flushed an otter—a commotion and a slight snort on the bank beside us. I could only see the undergrowth shaking, but Ricky had a clear look at it. So that made three since Lake Waccamaw; not exactly a multitude, but it did add up to two more otters than I had ever seen in all my boyhood years of knocking around on this river. Added to the beaver and the beaver-sign, the wood-duck, alligators, osprey, and deer I had encountered, the otters gave me the wholly unexpected impression that the river possessed a more abundant wildlife than it had twenty-five or thirty years earlier. Ricky suggested that this might simply reflect the massive development in the eastern part of the country; the Waccamaw swamps were among the last undisturbed habitats in their part of the world, and what we were seeing might be basically a population of refugees, augmented by eager beavers from the snowbelt.

But there was something else to it. The one form of local fauna that I had failed to find in anything like its former abundance was the river rat. There had been the trotliner above Little Savannah, and the shad fisherman whose encampment we had passed in review at the Needle's Eye, and that was it. On the river I remembered, such a spell of spring weather as we had had would have brought out men and boys in small plank or plywood boats; you would have seen them kicking along up river with a five-horse outboard, or slipping along in little one-man boats, hugging the bank, passing silently in and out of the shadows of overhanging trees. The river rats were deeply indigenous; they had about them the air of unhurried purpose that characterizes those things which belong to a landscape because they function in it. They might be tending a few shad nets, or drifting for shad with a seine or bow net, or they might be setting out trotlines. They might also have more furtive purposes in mind but out of sight: a fish-trap set back in a swampy creek, or a baited summer duck hole, where the duck would pile in just before dark, squealing and splashing like skinny dippers, and one double-barreled volley would harvest half a dozen of them.

At every landing along the river in those days there would be tethered a small cluster of the little locally made flat-bottomed boats, and those boats belonged specifically and exclusively to that particular landing. If you tried, as my father had once or twice, to leave your own boat there for a few weeks, when that section was at the right stage for fishing, you would return and find it sunk, if you found it at all, and when you finally pulled it out, you would find why it sank—a neat row of twenty-two holes stitched across the bottom, or one side of the fish-box bashed in. Each stretch of the river was possessively held, and the holders did what they could to discourage all forms of outside competition, from man or beast. Their attitude toward almost any creature they found along the river was that if it was not edible or otherwise useful, then it was probably a varmint and ought to be shot. This was less a reflection of a frontier mentality than of the remorseless practicality bred by a hard agricultural existence, in which you are at war with Nature, hoeing, chopping, cutting, girdling, grubbing, poisoning, and burning, from one end of the year to the other. The easy freedom of an otter, whether or not that otter ate the fish you might have caught, or robbed your nets, was of itself an affront, almost a blasphemy, in the way that an open and unapologetic sexual promiscuity would have been. The animal flouted the sweat of man's brow and the logic of a world that had been cursed for mankind's sake.

But now there were fewer farms and fewer farmers; the river rat was going the way of the mule, the paddling boat, and the cane pole. Everywhere through the country, you saw the empty houses in the middle of fields, doors and windows gone, disappearing under honeysuckle and catbriar. In the long run, development and gentrification might pose a more serious threat for wildlife than any number of lawless locals. But in the short run, the Waccamaw was probably a safer place for otters and alligators than it had been in my youth. An indulgent attitude toward wildlife does not flourish in a subsistence economy; it is almost a nostalgia, a luxury of civilization.

When we got back to the river proper the sun was low. The air was utterly still, and any sound, even the faint click of the paddle shaft against the gunwale, was strangely magnified. The Waccamaw was a broad silver reach before us, but it was time to make time now. Soon the beacons of the channel markers would be flashing. The river bent slightly westward and here at last, after so many miles of one river, was Bull Creek, full of piedmont clay, pouring its yellow water into the black Waccamaw. The two streams keep apart for a while, Bull Creek hugging the western bank, and the Waccamaw holding to the east. But gradually the two waters roil together in dissolving clouds, like milk in coffee, resolve themselves into something the color of chocolate, and give up their differences.

We were going to leave the Waccamaw now, for purely practical reasons. The most direct and prettiest way to Georgetown lay up Bull Creek, through Little Bull, and into the Pee Dee. Bishop had taken this route; anybody in a small boat would. But there is something else to it. At this point, where Bull Creek dumps into it, the Waccamaw River begins to drown. Bull is the first of the cut-through creeks from the Pee Dee, and these creeks divert the water from a tremendous watershed into the Waccamaw. The Big Pee Dee, assimilating the Yadkin, the Lynches, the Little Pee Dee, and the Lumber, rises in western North Carolina, at the base of Grandfather Mountain; its tributaries drain north-central South Carolina and a great part of the long southern edge of North Carolina. Technically, it flows into the Waccamaw, but that is only because the Waccamaw is lower. If you looked at a map showing the whole Pee Dee system spread out like a tree, rooted in Winyah Bay, fanning out through the Carolinas, and reaching as high as the eastern slope of the Appalachians, then the Waccamaw would appear as a peculiar, comparatively short branch that forks off at a right angle quite close to the ground.

Rivers are standard historical metaphors, and certainly the Waccamaw—a peculiarly situated tributary meandering with such convoluted deliberations that you could, in its upper reaches, begin to ask yourself whether it really meant to get anywhere or not—reflects the outwardly uneventful and peripheral history of the people who have lived along it. Nothing precipitous happens in the history or the river; there are no falls, no rapids, no watershed events. Before the Intracoastal Waterway Canal was completed, and could serve as a spillway, Conway was literally a backwater—when the Pee Dee was in flood, it would bring the Waccamaw to a standstill, then overflow into it, and yellow Pee Dee water would reach as far up as Kingston Lake.

Of course the arrangement of these rivers wasn't simply a metaphor of history; it was also a determining fact of history. The Waccamaw led nowhere but back into its own isolated swamps.

Watching it disappearing beneath the Pee Dee while still retaining the name of Waccamaw, I thought how that pretty well emblemized what had happened to the county in Ricky's and my lifetimes—it had gotten lost in something bigger; it still had its name, but was now indistinguishable within the vast influx of the present. There was no point in sentiment—no point in turning around and going back upstream a ways and collecting a jar full of unadulterated Waccamaw water to carry with us for luck. Water in a jar is water in a jar. We turned up into Bull Creek. The canoe yawed a bit as the heavy current struck against the bow, but we got her straightened out and pushed her hard, needing to find a campsite while there was still light.

Strictly speaking, I had been trespassing every night of my trip, pitching my tent and cooking my supper without authorization, on land that belonged to somebody else. But I had felt secure in doing it—on the upper and middle Waccamaw, something of the old, unwritten tradition of the riparian rights of fishermen, hunters, trappers, log-rafters, and other casual users still survives. In the lower river there had never been any such tradition. For more than two centuries, Georgetown County river frontage (and, until 1865, a high percentage of the people inhabiting it) had been property zealously kept and guarded. Mr. Wilson Edge never ran his hogs in these swamps; in his day, most of the Georgetown County swamps had long since been cleared, drained, and diked, so that the river itself could not enter them without permission. In the middle of Bull Creek, with Horry County to the right of us and Georgetown County to the left of us, Ricky and I had a choice of very clear legal, if not moral, implication. We could sleep on the Horry Country side, where there was a good clay bank, and where we would disturb no one and no one would disturb us. Or we could sleep on the other side, on Sandy Island, and hope not to be discovered.

Sandy Island is formed by Bull and Thoroughfare creeks, to the north and south, and the Waccamaw and Pee Dee rivers, to the east and west. It is roughly six miles long and three miles wide. It includes a good deal of swampland, but most of it is what the name implies. It appears to be a range of coastal dunes that got left behind and slowly went to seed. The history of its ownership is long and complicated; neither of us knew who held it at present. But it had always been an emphatically private place, one that was rumored to be patrolled by a caretaker not noted for amiability. In our high school days, we had been ashore a few times—at Mount Arena, a small black village downriver, on the Waccamaw, and at the Thoroughfare end, where a fine sand bluff drops into the creek. And we had passed by the Bull Creek end often enough to know that it was as handsome a place as existed anywhere on the river, or anywhere in the world we knew.

For the first mile up Bull Creek, Sandy Island was swampy, and then we came to what we were looking for—a sandy bluff, crowned with longleaf pines. The last of the afternoon sun was glinting on the surface of the water, and reflecting horizontal bands of rippling light up into the trees, but it seemed as though the trees were pulsing a soft, diffused light out of themselves, like embers. There was no need to go through the formality of a discussion. We sat for a moment looking at the island, then paddled in along the shore. For decency's sake, we went a few hundred yards beyond a sign that promised the full pain and penalty of the law for trespassers.

It was awkward work getting our gear up the bluff. At the top, we found ourselves in an airy and open woods, densely carpeted with pinestraw. Standing amid our gear, we could see perhaps a quarter of a mile across undulating sandy ridges, broken here and there by little swale-like bays. Like all long-leaf pines, these were as straight and limbless as palm trees, all the way up to the crown. They were uniform in size, and each stood distinct and apart, with a certain sort of dignified reserve. A few scrub oaks—turkey oak, Ricky said—were scattered through the understory of the pines. Behind us the river glittered, but it seemed removed from us, as though its glare were outside, and we were inside, in a hushed room full of softened light. A small road, no more than a sandy track, led back into the interior of the island.

We set about our business, I to cook and Ricky to gather firewood. I cleared away the straw—it was nearly a foot deep, and because the sand under it held no moisture, it was as dry and undecayed as cured hay—and started the stove. Ricky, using a pulaski—a double-bitted tool, axe on one side, grubbing hoe on the other—set to work on a little dead oak. The noise of his chopping, like the light, seemed filtered and muted, strangely remote. It cooled off fast as the sun dropped and the evening chill, held back all day by the sun, crept up from the river and the swamps. Ricky came up and dumped an armful of wood. Turkey oak is sorry stuff, an arboreal weed, but the heartwood was startlingly vivid, a grainy scarlet, and Ricky's axe-work was neat and smooth, as tidy as I could have done with a chisel. He went off again and came back with a chunk of pine, rotten and crumbling on the outside, and a tallowy orange inside: fat lightwood (liter'd), he announced with satisfaction. Supper was underway now—steak, okra, and potatoes, sizzling and steaming, and I watched him start the lightwood, the black pitch running out of the wood as it caught and falling in flaming droplets to the sand. He added a few pine cones—big longleaf cones, almost the size of footballs—and then the oak, and soon the fire was snapping at the chill air. As soon as there is a good fire to look at, the world away from the fire seems to grow darker and colder, even a dog feels that, and gives up its venturesomeness, and draws close to the flame, as though suddenly afraid of what might be out there in the night. We got the tent up in a hurry, and then sat with whiskey, and watched the sun set over the swamps that lay across Bull Creek.

We ate. Eating on camping trips is seldom as leisurely as you feel it should be—there is always the fire to tend or mosquitoes or weather to worry you—but nothing disturbs the methodical

159

tranquility of Ricky McIver with a plateful of food. When we were boys he enjoyed a certain fame for the way he would sit down to the plate before him, and first eat all of whatever happened to be on the side of the plate nearest to his mouth. When he had finished, let's say, the sweet potatoes, he would rotate the plate 72° and begin on the collards; then another 72° and on to the pork chops; after which, careful as a helmsman changing course, he would rotate it again, bringing the biscuits into alignment, and after that the field peas. If someone addressed a remark to him while he was lifting the fork to his mouth, he would look directly at them, the fork suspended between mouth and plate, until the remark was finished. Then, depending on the interest of the remark or the degree of rumination it required, he would either raise the fork the rest of the way to his mouth, and chew the food over as carefully as though it were a proposition that had been put to him, and then respond: "Pretty well, thank you ma'am," or "I guess so." Or he would carefully replace the fork, still loaded with food, on the plate, and say what he had to say, and then pick it up and start it toward his mouth again. Here, sitting propped against a tree beside the fire, he ate rather more randomly and briskly than in those days, but still with a craftsman's serious and unhurried concentration on the job at hand.

As we had paddled down from Conway, talking, telling stories, recalling expeditions to this or that section of the river, it occurred to me that we were beginning to sound like old-timers. As boys, we'd listened to Mr. McIver, Daddy, and a lot of other men talk about fishing and hunting, or somebody's bone-headed bird dog or self-willed Model A roadster. They were all men who had been in the war, and there would be glimpses of military life, almost always funny. We had knocked around on our own, in small boats, first on Kingston Lake, which we could reach by walking, and then, as we got up into high school, on the Waccamaw. Neither of us had much aptitude for the social life of high school, and Ricky did not even pretend to. I kept waiting on a story to happen to me. None did, confirming my sense that there was nothing to do but try to make myself into a plausible imitation of a member of my own generation. I stood on the sidelines at school dances, and played basketball with vehement ineptitude. Ricky kept wholly apart from all that; it was as though, from a very early age, he had more strenuous things to think about. He worked in his father's warehouse on Saturday mornings, and spent a lot of time in the Kingston Lake swamps, which lay just across the street from his house.

High schools don't value independence, and he did not have an easy time of it. His teachers found him stubborn, unless they could persuade him of the utility of what they were teaching. Mathematics and science were fine; he had no use for Latin, and no power under heaven could persuade him that the correct form of a footnote was a thing that any self-respecting human being would condescend to learn. His classmates, even in Conway, thought of him as a rustic—angular, deliberate, with a certain ineradicable formality about him. Until we reached high school, he refused to wear shoes, winter or summer, except on Sunday. On both sides, his family were ultimately from Scotland, and manifested that tenacious sense of national identity so characteristic of transplanted Scots men and women. Many of the Highland stereotypes seemed to fulfill themselves in him. He accepted his own singularity as a matter of fact and maintained it as a matter of honor; expected life to be a test of principle and toughness, and was indifferent to opinion.

Our friendship had never seemed remarkable; it has never come up for discussion. With our mutual cousin Sam Dargan, we went off to college together, to Sewanee, in East Tennessee. Ricky took one look at the incredible flora of the Cumberland plateau and majored in forestry, while I chose literature. In theory, his discipline was exact, definite, and unadventurous; mine, in theory, involved daily ventures out upon strange seas of thought, alone. In practice, it went entirely the other way. Literature led me, predictably and without interruption, from college to graduate school and from graduate school to college teaching and from there, presumably, to eternity. In his college summers, Ricky fought forest fires out West, and after college, he rattled around a bit— a year of graduate work in forestry at Duke, and then a year of teaching high school chemistry, at some peril to himself and his students, in Georgetown.

The year after that, while I was occasionally stopping on the steps of Widener library to listen to intense young men haranguing small clots of mildly interested undergraduates about genocide, imperialism, and napalm, Ricky resumed postgraduate education, this time at Quantico, Virginia. He graduated second lieutenant, USMC, and shipped out to Vietnam. In the middle of a balmy spring night in 1967, I got a telephone call from our old college classmate, Dick Nowlin, from his home in Minnesota. Dick had just heard that Ricky had stepped on a mine, was still alive, and was scheduled for evacuation. That was all he knew. We talked about it as people do—calmly and numbly. No, it didn't seem, from our dim conception of the thing, that there would be much life left to anyone who had stepped on a mine—certainly not much of what Ricky himself would consider life.

I spent the rest of that night walking around Cambridge, and called Mrs. McIver as early as I dared to the next morning. She answered on the first ring. None of the McIvers had ever lacked composure or fortitude, and her voice was almost perfectly steady. Two marines, in their dress uniforms, had brought the telegram yesterday—no, day before yesterday it was. It was a form telegram, the information typed in: where wounded, how wounded, nature and extent of injuries, and prognosis. He was wounded in the head, right arm, and right leg. The prognosis said "Good," and the two marines told her that if it said good it meant good. So she permitted herself a light little laugh, that overtook a choking in the throat: "I'd worry about that *head* wound, but you know how hard that rascal's head is. His father says he gets it from me;

I say he gets it from him, and we can argue about it for an hour at the time, so I guess we're *both* right." He would be evacuated to Japan, they told her, and she might hope to hear from him soon.

By early summer he had been brought back to the naval hospital in Charleston, and I visited him there. He had lost the little finger on his right hand and was on crutches. His skull had been fractured, and repaired by a steel plate. He was invincible: "I take con-SID'able satisfaction in that steel plate—the first McIver with a skull of *re-inforced* cement." He was already able to peg around the hospital on crutches, and he took me through the ward, introducing me to other casualities, several of them men from his own unit. By the end of the summer he was out of the hospital. His wound was serious enough to disqualify him for further active service, and he completed his military career stateside.

His war wasn't a war for big stories of the kind we used to hear, and he didn't talk much about it. He had volunteered out of conviction, and the conviction hadn't survived what he had seen there. But it also seemed to me that his volunteering came out of something deeper in him, and that did not change. It was as though he had a frustration with the world of talk and speculation, where convictions and opinions ebbed and flowed, were exchanged and negotiated as though they meant no more than the play money in a game of Monopoly. He always looked for the hard currency of action and risk, and that took him, once his term of service was done, out to Montana, to become a smoke jumper in the United States Forest Service. By this time, I had settled in Maine; we would see each other in Conway, every other year or so. In winters, he found a variety of jobs—worked with an old friend down in New Orleans, helped out in his father's lumberyard in Conway, or on his cousin's farm over in Darlington, which was the ancestral stronghold, at least on this side of the Atlantic, of clan McIver. But with the spring he would head back out to Montana and the smoke jumping. It is a young man's profession, but he kept at it into his forties and the beginning of gray hair; through marriage, children, divorce; remarriage, more children.

And then the previous summer he had landed in a pile of fallen timber, and ruined his right knee. With a brace, he could get around pretty well, but there was no question of his jumping again, and, as far as he was concerned, no question of his accepting the desk job that was offered to him, which would have kept him in the Forest Service long enough to qualify for a pension. He had come back to Conway, and was working in the lumberyard again. We had talked about it today, as we paddled. He and his father always seemed to accept each other's firmness of purpose and uncompromising individuality with perfect equanimity, neither one of them expecting the other to alter course or take in sail. It wasn't at all clear that they were going to be able to function as partners, or that Ricky had any other options available. "Quite an accomplishment, to have reached my age without having acquired a marketable skill," he said, and then he had put his paddle down and twisted around to look at me, and grinned: "But I can't complain. I've had a forty-year boyhood."

After we finished supper, Ricky built the fire up. This seemed to me imprudent, considering that we were trespassers, but prudence had never been one of his strong suits. Then we made ourselves comfortable again. There was nothing more to do, and we were lazy or shy enough to let Bull Creek supply whatever profundity the occasion required. Its name suggests its size and force— a bull of a creek in the daylight, brown, turbid, swirling heavily around its bends and against its banks; and an even bullier creek in the darkness, leadenly reflecting the night sky and sending its vapors inland. It was easy to see how people had imagined these vapors to be pestilential—nineteenth-century science verifying much older fears of what lurked in swamps, bogs, and fens.

Our talk wandered around through news, gossip, politics, and returned again and again to landscapes and particular places. Ricky had seen much of the West, having fought fires from Alaska to

New Mexico. I asked him what place of the ones he'd seen he liked best. He laughed. "I used to think that way all the time. Land of heart's desire. Play games with myself about what square mile of real estate I would choose to own if the choice was mine. You can drive yourself crazy that way." He stopped and thought, and became deliberate. "There's more to any one good place than you could ever take in in one lifetime, and every new place you see makes you appreciate something else about the ones you already know. I never knew until I went to Montana how much I liked the Southern hardwoods. Even stuff like those water oaks and laurel oaks we passed today. Worthless, but there isn't a prettier tree in the spring, when it's coming into leaf."

I ventured that every trip always seemed to be just a scouting trip; you always told yourself that someday you would come back, with all the time in the world, and dig in, and see the seasons through. Ricky chewed on that a while. "Our children aren't going to feel that way. There won't be many places left, and you'll have to pay to see them. I don't mean just wilderness. I mean even the places we used to knock around—Kingston Lake or Little Savannah. Too many people, too much money at stake. People in Conway right now will pay about anything to live on the river, and once they've paid it, they aren't going to let just any ordinary joker go camping or squirrel hunting in the backyard. If I tried to take Lucas camping or hunting around Conway right now, I couldn't be sure that somebody wouldn't come out and run us off. He isn't going to grow up knowing much about any real place." He laughed. "Maybe people will be better off that way, better adjusted. But I don't envy them."

As we had come down the river today, we'd stopped more than once for him to investigate a shrub, methodically checking out the botanical keys, perhaps chewing a leaf or twig, until he had satisfied himself as to what it was. His patient passion for vegetation was unlikely in so rugged and adventurous a character as he had turned out to be. Seeing him at work around his house, transplanting flowers, or, after careful deliberation, setting out a white oak seedling that he had dug from the swamps, and that would still be a seedling after he had pulled up stakes and gone elsewhere, I could sense the conflicts that were in him. He had always been one to push his own convictions to the limit, or, as it had sometimes seemed, to let them carry him beyond any possibility of finding a tolerable compromise with the world of his own time. His tendency to see things in terms of stark and simple oppositions did not alter the fact that he was a complex man, with a wider range of experiences and aptitudes, and a more original way of reflecting upon them, than almost anybody I knew. His life needed a wide margin, but here he was, an endangered species, running out of habitat.

I stood up to stir the fire and saw, wavering through the woods behind us, the headlights of a truck. No point in trying to cover the fire now; we'd surely been spotted. Ricky looked up and swore. "All he can do is run us off," I said, and Ricky said for me to talk to him, that he wasn't up to contrition at the moment.

So I went out to the little sandy road and waited on the truck. It pulled up to me—I could see nothing beyond its headlights—and stopped about fifteen feet away. It sat there idling for a moment, then the driver cut the engine, but he left the lights on—wanting, I supposed, to be sure that we didn't try to run off or do anything drastic. Finally the door creaked open and he got out, but I still couldn't see anything beyond the glare of the lights. In such a situation, you expect someone big and burly and gruff, but the voice that issued out of the darkness was mild, more querulous than angry: "Now you boys ain't supposed to be here. I don't have to tell you that."

I said no sir, he didn't have to tell us that. We were just canoeing and needed a place to camp for the night.

He had by this time emerged into the headlights, and I could see what I was dealing with. He was a big man and an old one—

wrinkled, wearing a plaid lumber jacket buttoned tight around his neck, a wool cap, and gold-rimmed spectacles, through which he regarded me steadily.

"Well, now. You can't stay here. This land's posted, and I got to run you off." He sounded apologetic about it. I couldn't do much but agree with him and ask him if he knew anyplace where we might camp. He didn't answer that, but asked who we were and where we were from. When I told him my name, and that I was from Conway, he said, "Now your Daddy would be the lawyer?"

"That's right."

"Well. Me and your Daddy was in school together, right there in Conway. I knowed your uncle better than I did him; we done a right smart of survey work together, back before the war. Mr. Jack. He died some little time ago, didn't he?"

"Yes sir. 1953."

"How about your Daddy. He still keepin' right on?"

"Keepin' right on."

"Well I'm glad to hear it. When you see him, ast him does he remember Lonnie Cartrette. I believe it's forty years since I seen him. But I speck he remembers me."

Ricky got up and came over. Ricky's immediate family being from Darlington County, Mr. Cartrette did not know them, but he knew who Mr. McIver was: "Runs that lumberyard in Conway, don't he? I sold him some fine cypress logs one time. Fifteen cent a foot. Don't seem possible now, but it was a right handsome price then." The subject of our expulsion seemed to have been tabled. He turned off the headlights and we went over and stood by the fire. He said nothing for a while, just stood with his back to the fire. Finally, he looked at us: "Like I say, you boys got to leave. But you ain't got to leave this minute. You go ahead and spend the night here, and slip off early in the morning. Ain't no harm in that."

We thanked him. Ricky told him we'd just finished our supper, but we could offer him some ginger snaps and a cup of coffee. He declined, but took the invitation kindly, and we all sat down. As is often the case with people who choose to live in some degree of physical isolation, he was eager to talk; at one point he stopped and looked at us very earnestly and said, "Now you boys don't let me talk too much. Just say the word and I'll stop." But neither of us felt any inclination to say the word.

"I've spent a good many nights right here, sleeping and waiting on the turn of the tide, so I could get a load of logs down to Waccamaw on the slack water, and then take 'em up to Conway on the rise. Ain't a nicer spot on the whole river.

"Now I warn't no reg'lar logger. Made my living farming, over by Pawley Swamp. My folks had a place there. But you can't count on farming to do much more than keep you alive in a bad year, and two bad years in a row'll put you so far behind you won't never get caught up. So when I had a good year, I bought me a boat and a big winch. Made a platform with pontoon floaters, held together by oak stringers. Sixteen foot square. I did my logging underwater."

The boat had an inboard engine, and he towed the platform behind him. The winch was mounted over the middle of the platform. When he got over a log, he would use the winch to lower down a big set of tongs, like those you see on a lumber truck. He would grope deep in the current with his iron hand until the tongs had a sure grip, then he would winch the log up and secure it, slinging ropes under it so that it rode between the pontoons. Ricky asked him how he knew where the log lay.

"I had me a pike·about thirty foot long with a iron head on her. I'd proge along the bottom 'till I hit something solid; then I'd jab it a few more times to be sure it was sound and figure out how it was lying. I got so I could tell pine from cypress, just by jabbing. You jab hard into it, and it if was pine, they'd come up a few little spots of turpentine. Looked like somebody spilt a drop of gasoline on the water.

"Sometimes it would be one log, and sometimes it would be a bundle of 'em. When you fell a cypress, you got to sling it between two big pine logs. Green cypress won't float no more than a lead pipe. Sometimes they'd miscalc'late, and the whole thing would sink. It used to tickle me to think of 'em cussing when they finally got them logs to the river and got'em slung together, and then had the whole thing to sink on 'em." He had a light little giggle, as though he were too polite to laugh, and he giggled now at the recollection on how one generation's improvidence provided him with a waterlogged windfall.

"A great big log down in the mud, you couldn't hoist it with the winch. So I'd wait on the low tide and then winch it as tight as I could. When the tide started to rising it was a tug a' war, and that raft would set in the river like it had growed roots. But finally—pop!—the log would break aloose from the bottom and that raft would bounce right up like a cork. Then it warn't no trouble to winch it on up. Biggest log I ever struck was 1952, right down there by Bates Hill Plantation. I knowed they done a lot of cutting in there, way back; used to be a tramroad come down to the river there. So it stood to reason. It took me the longest time to get it up. Twenty-four foot long. They was doin' some dredgin' at the time in at Bates Hill, and we tried to get it out on the bank with a dredge and a dragline, but it didn't work. I wound up taking it to Port Harrelson. Had a friend there with a big caterpillar tractor. He got it about halfway up the bank so we could cut it in two. Then he put it on a flatbed truck. He couldn't take but one section at a time. You don't see no more trees like that."

But usually he would deliver the logs directly to the mill himself, to save carrying costs. His boat had a twelve-horse, one-lung motor—no speed but plenty of power. He'd deliver to either Conway or Georgetown, depending on where the prices were higher. Georgetown was easy—he'd drop down the Pee Dee to Thoroughfare Creek, the next cut-through below Bull Creek, and then go on down the Waccamaw to Georgetown. Getting a load of logs to Conway from the Pee Dee was a different matter. "My boat couldn't pull against the current when the tide was running strong. So I'd want rising water to get to Conway. But the trickiest part was Little Bull Creek." Little Bull leaves the Pee Dee below Bull Creek, and it connects to Bull Creek about two miles above where Bull empties into the Waccamaw. It is narrow and sinuous. The Pee Dee is slightly more elevated than the Waccamaw, and so the water flows down through Little Bull except at the very peak of the tide, when it comes briefly to a standstill and then sluggishly reverses itself. "It snakes around so much you couldn't tow nothing through there with the current behind you—it would swing the raft into the bushes every time. So you had to wait on the slack water to start, and you couldn't rush it. It hept a little when the tide swung—it wurn't strong enough to stop you, and it kept the raft straight out behind. It ever'thing went right you'd get to big Bull about the start of the ebb, and take her down to Waccamaw. And then it wurn't a thing in this world to do but tie up and wait on rising water. Many's the night I anchored the raft down there in the river, and come back up here in my boat, and tied her up, and cooked me some supper right here on this hill, and maybe slep a little. But when that tide changed, you wanted to be all hooked up and ready to go, even if it was the middle of the night. Lose a tide, and you might be two days just getting to Conway."

He stopped and looked at us. "I told you boys not to let me talk too much," he said. "I'm right deaf now, and a deaf man always talks too much, so he don't have to try and listen. It gets to be a habit." This surprised me. He spoke very softly, something I did not associate with old people whose hearing had gone, but it explained the intensity with which he peered at each of us whenever we asked him a question or made a comment. He did that now as we assured him that we'd enjoyed listening, but he said it was bedtime anyway; he needed to get on back to his cabin. He got up and brushed off his pants. "Look. You'll be wantin' to start early tomorrow. Don't fool with cookin' no breakfast. I ain't no fancy cook, but I can fix you some breakfast." We of course said oh no we couldn't do that; he said, with his mild laugh, that we'd better remember we were trespassers, "and you ain't got no choice in the matter." So it ended that he would come pick us up and give us some breakfast first thing in the morning.

He was as good as his word—we were just out of the tent and a whitish mist hung low among the trees when his truck hove into view. I let Ricky ride in front and made myself comfortable in back. Warblers were beginning to stir in the treetops, and the crowns of the pines caught the first light of the sun. We lurched slowly through longleaf and scrub oak, and down into little bays and branches that spread a few inches of black water across the road, and packed it smooth and hard as a beach at low tide. The cabin itself stood on pilings beside Cooter Creek, a long bayou that runs through the middle of Sandy Island. It was built, Mr. Cartrette told us, to serve as a clubhouse for the men who owned the island, so it was rather more than a caretaker's shack. There was a pleasant porch and a big, nicely panelled room, where eight or ten people could have been comfortable, with a fireplace at one end and a fine modern kitchen at the other. Mr. Cartrette already had breakfast cooked—sausage, grits, eggs, pancakes, and coffee strong enough to wake the dead. We ate and talked. I asked him how he came to have his present job.

"Fellow before me didn't like it over here. Got lonely. He'd go off to the mainland whenever he thought wouldn't nobody notice, and when he was here he mostly just set around inside and watched the television. So I heard they was looking for a replacement. My wife had died and my boys had all growed up and moved away. I couldn't be no lonelier here than setting at home. People don't like to talk to no deaf man. I always did like the swamp and the river, so I sold the farm and come on over here. It don't pay a whole lot, but I got me enough money saved up to live the way I want to for as long as a man's got any right to live. They let me fish and hunt all I want to, but mostly I just like to watch. It's wildcat and turkeys and deer over here, about everything you could think of. I put out feed for the turkeys; some mornings they're out scratching around the house like a bunch of chickens."

We finished eating and moved out onto the porch and sat to talk a little longer, while the sunlight worked its way down the trees toward the water, still lying inky-black in shadow. I was wondering to myself how a man ever managed to make enough money out of farming and timber salvage to be able to save anything, and Mr. Cartrette seemed to guess my thought. He had been picking his teeth; now he spat out the toothpick:

"Best thing ever happened to me was when they decided to put in a community well at Bucksville. I'd got about all the logs I was going to get out of the Pee Dee, so I sold my outfit and bought myself a drillin' rig. When they set the job at Bucksville out to contract, I didn't get it. 'Was my bid too high?' I ast'em. 'No,' they said, 'we just don't think you got the equipment and the know-how to do it.' So they hired a big outfit from Columbia.

"Well sir, them fellows from Columbia set right down there in Bucksville for two solid year, drilling one hole after another, and every hole nine hundred or a thousand foot deep. Not a drop in any of them. The usual drillin' contract is you get paid so much per gallon to the minute. After two years, the company sued the community; said they brought 'em down there to drill where it wurn't no water, and they had to cover expenses. So I went to 'em in Bucksville again. 'Look,' I said, 'you let me drill. If I find water, the company ain't got no case against you.' 'What'll you charge?' they said. 'Ten thousand dollars for every hundred gallons to the minute.' 'What if you don't find no water?' 'You won't owe me a cent.'

"I told 'em the only thing I ast was the right to set the hole where I wanted it, and not where no geologist told me. 'Suit your-sef,' they said; 'it ain't no skin offen our nose.' My first hole was eight hundred foot and it yelt five hundred gallons to the minute.

It was water everywhere down there, but you got to know where to place your screens to let it in. With my little rig I could listen to the engine and tell when she was drillin' rock and when she was drillin' mud. Them big rigs was so powerful it all sounded the same, mud or rock.

"Well, after that, I was drilling everywhere, Georgia to Virginia, and I made me a pile of money. Last well I done was over to the beach. Man I was working for over there says, 'Don't guess you'd ever sell that rig, would you?' I said I'd sell anything if I got my price. 'Cause I seen I had as much money as I was going to need. So I told him seventy-five thousand dollars and he bought it on the spot. 'At least let me finish out this hole for you before you buy it,' I said, but he said no, he'd buy it right there, then he'd pay me a wage to work for him until the well was dug, so he could learn how to do it. So we finished out, and I taken the money and quit. I hear he ain't done so well as he hoped with the drillin'. Seems like there's considerable art to it, same as anything else. It don't do to trust to no luck."

It would be a pleasure, back in Maine, to think of Mr. Cartrette spending his days here on Sandy Island. He read a little, he said, and sometimes tried to watch television, but it was all silliness. Mostly he liked to drive the length and breadth of Sandy Island, seeing what he could see. He carried a serviceable-looking old twelve-gauge double barrel in the truck with him, to show to trespassers and poachers. They didn't give him a great deal of back-talk. It was a nice, quiet job—lonely sometimes, but then life was lonely anywhere when your children had grown up and moved out and your wife had died and silence had started to close in around you. The swamp and pine woods were full of interest to him—he drove us around before delivering us back to the tent; showed us an old Indian site, where there were shards of pottery, took us down toward the south end, where big live oaks and scattered brickwork marked all that was left of Pipe Down plantation, one of the two that had been on Sandy Island. He pointed out

173

the faint bed of an old tramroad, pines scarred by turpentining operations a century ago, and turkey tracks everywhere in the sand. For all the talking he did, he did not seem like a talkative man—he spoke slowly and softly, like someone who had thought a good deal about things, but who wasn't in the habit of publicizing his discoveries, and didn't have the phrases ready-formed. But in listening to him, you felt no deficiency in his language. It was very much of a piece with him, practical, deliberate, and apt.

# 6  In the Land of the Rice Planter

By nine o'clock, we were back on the water. We continued on
Bishop's course, paddling up against the heavy current of Bull Creek,
holding to the eddies as much as we could. It was a bright, clear
morning; the oaks were softly vivid in the swamps. About a mile
up Bull from our campsite, Little Bull gave off to the left, and we
entered its twisting channel. It was narrow; the swamp, closing in
on both banks, had a decidedly jungle-like quality. On the second
corner of Little Bull, we surprised two alligators, five or six feet
long; they surged into the water just ahead of us, close enough
for their wake to rock the canoe. But Little Bull was more notable
for a large, mixed flock of snowy egrets and white ibis in the
crown of an enormous laurel oak. They took flight—the egrets
silently, the ibis with muted, worried gutturals. The egrets flew
directly off; the ibis circled over the oak until they had marshalled
themselves into a regular flock. Against the deep blue of the sky,
they were stunningly white, except for the jet of the wingtips and
the strange, featherless red faces. Their elegantly decurved beaks
and the stiff angularity of their extended necks and feet made
them look radically stylized, like something destined for or escaped

from a hieroglyph. Their flight was duck-like, direct and purposeful, as though they intended to go a long way, but we came upon them twice more before we got out of Little Bull, scattered like laundry in the treetops, where they seemed to have an aptitude for the heraldic pose. That, combined with their glaring whiteness, isolated them from the scene; I know of no bird that seems, while in its natural environment, so apart from nature, so much like a silhouette or icon. Later in the day we saw a flock of perhaps a hundred of them soaring over the marshes, all wheeling in a stately counterclockwise rotation. This is a habit with them, and it has no apparent purpose, nothing to do with feeding or nesting or diurnal migration. They strongly resemble the sacred ibis of the Nile, and it is easy to persuade yourself that this flight has a priestly character, and enacts some cosmic mystery.

The ibis did portend, more clearly than any single thing, that I had now entered the last part of my trip. I have never seen an ibis in the Waccamaw above Bull Creek. They feed in marshes, and belong altogether to that section of the river which is still called the ricefields, although it has been more than a century since rice grew there in any quantity. Sandy Island is the last piece of high land between the Waccamaw and the Pee Dee, as they move toward their final confluence in Winyah Bay. From Thoroughfare Creek, at the south end of Sandy Island, it is about twelve miles to where the rivers join. The narrowing wedge of land between them was once filled with towering cypress and gum and veined with the creeks—Guendalose, Squirrel, Schooner, Jericho—that progressively siphon off the Pee Dee into the Waccamaw. As Ricky and I descended the Pee Dee, we would be paddling down a stream that shrank until it was a river in name only. By the time it joins the Waccamaw, it has frittered away its inheritance, and is no bigger than any of a dozen ricefield creeks.

Bishop had had the benefit of the freshet all the way down from Lake Waccamaw, and he paid the cost of it in Bull and Little Bull: "At times the boat would not move a hundred feet in five minutes, and often, as my strength seemed failing me, I caught the friendly branches of trees, and held on to keep the canoe from being whirled down the current towards the Waccamaw." But he eventually made the Pee Dee:

> The paper canoe had now reached the regions of the riceplanter. Along the low banks of the Pee Dee were diked marshes where, before the civil war, each estate produced from five thousand to forty thousand bushels of rice annually, and the lords of rice were more powerful than those of cotton, though cotton was king. The rich lands here produced as high as fifty-five bushels of rice to the acre, under forced slave labor; now the free blacks cannot wrest from nature more than twenty-five or thirty bushels.
>
> Fine old mansions line the river's banks, but the families had been so reduced by the ravages of war, that I saw refined ladies, who had been educated in the schools of Edinburgh, Scotland, overseeing the negroes as they worked in the yards of the rice-mills. The undaunted spirit of those southern ladies, as they worked in their homes now so desolate, roused my admiration.
>
> A light, graceful figure, enveloped in an old shawl, and mounted

on an old horse, flitted about one plantation like a restless spirit.

"That lady's father," said a gentleman to me, "owned three plantations, worth three millions of dollars, before the war. There is a rice mill on one of the plantations worth thirty thousand dollars. She now fights against misfortune, and will not give up. The Confederate war would not have lasted six months if it had not been for our women. They drove thousands of us young men to the fight; and now, having lost all, they go bravely to work, even taking the places of their old servants in their grand old homes. It's hard for them, though, I assure you."

There is a good deal of the romance of the ricefields, and of the Lost Cause, which tended to personify itself in an idealized image of Southern womanhood, in this. But there is also a specific history which we are fortunate enough to know. The graceful figure that Bishop saw was Elizabeth Waites Allston Pringle, whose father, Robert Francis Withers Allston, owned five, rather than three, plantations, at one of which, Waverly, there was a steam-driven rice mill of advanced design. Bishop's seeing her brings the thread of his narrative across the thread of hers, for she too was a writer, and a very fine one. One has the sense, when this admirable Yankee looked upon a woman who was at least his match in intrepidity, modesty, and amiability, of two worlds drawn tantalizingly close to each other. Did she look up and see his strange craft passing? A little further downstream, Bishop would in fact stop in at Nightingale Hall, and there call on Elizabeth's brother, Colonel Benjamin Allston, but if Benjamin mentioned this encounter to Elizabeth at all, we have no record of it.

Their father, Robert Francis Withers Allston, had been among the wealthiest of the Georgetown District rice planters, who were, as a group, among the wealthiest people in the nation. But the computation of wealth is a curious business. This is from a letter to R. F. W. Allston from his mother, Charlotte Anne Allston, in 1819, when he was sixteen, and in his first year at West Point:

we are all ploding on here much at the same old rate Rice fell badly, and that depresses the spirits of the Majority of the People here, whose chief object is to make Rice to buy Negroes to make rice there is so much contention about property that it keeps Lawyers Busy, then sickness keeps the Doctors also Busy, but the Merchant can go occasionally to take a Game of Billiards, and not be Missed out of his stoar the markets are bad, no money, no money is the cry continually we had 112 barrels of Rice sold, which brought only $1012, which you know is not enough to pay Tax clothes Blankets, and shoes, besides Doctor Bills and other expencies how can we expect to live, what is to become of us this is what you have heard all your life my Dear Son, and it looks as if we are Doomed to live in this state of fear and hope which no Doubt is for the Best, if we had all we wished we would be too [illegible] and never think of another world, which we are doomed to, and ought to prepare for.

She had been a widow for eight years, was beleaguered by disease, litigation, debt, high water ("there is a great Fresh in Pee Dee from a deal of Rain we have had lately, how I shall get through these swamps I cant tell my poor old Horses hold out wonderfully, I much fear one day or other they will fail and leave me in the Road."), and as the tone, logic, and even the punctuation of her correspondence indicates, she seems to have been a person whose anxieties and unhappinesses fed upon themselves, compounded and proliferated until she could not tell where one worry ended and another began.

But while she may have been inclined to make the most of her worries, the worries themselves were neither inconsequential nor atypical. We hear them again and again—the anxiety over crops and prices, the shortage of ready cash, the enormous overhead costs of slavery, the continual litigation, the prevalence of diseases that rendered the lives of animals, slaves, and slave-owners almost equally uncertain. And, on top of this, there was the specific vulnerability of rice to the unpredictable "Fresh," or freshets, which, coming down either the Pee Dee or the Waccamaw, could not only wipe out a year's crop in a few hours, but could also, by destroying the elaborate system of dikes, ditches, and trunks, require huge outlays of money and labor.

In one half of her heart, his mother hoped that Robert F. W. Alston might ecape the ricelands altogether. She speaks of the possibility of his moving upcountry and becoming a cotton planter, or pursuing a profession. But one senses very strongly, in reading her unhappy letters to him, that she never really seriously conceived of his doing anything other than what he in fact did, when, at the age of twenty-one, he resigned his commission and came home to assume the life of a planter. He would have done so with open eyes and no delusions. The life of a planter was no mirage; his mother would have filled him with a sense of its perturbations and uncertainties.

Robert Allston survived the perilous climate; he married wisely and happily, bought and inherited additional riceland, much of it as yet uncleared. He was highly esteemed by those whose estimation mattered; he was successively elected to the state house, the state senate, and the governorship. With no pretenses to connoisseurship, he collected art and found deep satisfaction in it; despite all his business, he was able to take his family on an abbreviated European tour. The ideal of Cato the Elder and Cincinnatus—that of the farmer and private man who enters public life only from a sense of responsibility, and not from ambition—had descended to him, considerably softened, gentrified, and Christianized by the English eighteenth century; Fielding's Squire Allworthy stands just behind him.

To his daughter Elizabeth, who was to become the "light, graceful figure, enveloped in an old shawl and mounted on an old horse," he possessed precisely those qualities of patriarchal benevolence that he himself would have attributed to God. When she was about three, she stole a peach, denied it, and was willing to let a servant be blamed for it; but her father had seen her. He spoke methodically to her about the evil of theft, the greater evil of falsehood, and the greatest evil, a willingness to let an innocent person be punished in her stead. He sent her to her room:

> After a while my father came and gave me a severe switching. When he had finished he kissed me, put me on the bed, and threw a light coverlet over me, and I went to sleep. I slept a long time, for when I woke up it was nearly dark, and I felt like an angel in heaven—so happy and peaceful and, above all, filled with a kind of adoration for my father. It is strange what a realization of right and wrong that gave me, baby though I was.

A year or two later, the episode was repeated—transgression, punishment, sleep: "As before, I went to sleep on the little white bed and woke up feeling like an angel in heaven, with adoration in my heart for the God who had conquered the evil spirit which had possessed me." She looked back at those childhood scenes from her old age, a person who had experienced more than a lifetime's portion of loss: the dark days of '64 and '65, which saw the death of her father and the physical destruction of his world; a marriage which had made her "too happy to live, I often felt," and had left her a childless widow after only six years; her own heroic efforts, after her mother's death, to save the remaining fragment of a vast patrimony by growing rice in the old way, and the final destruction of that undertaking by the great hurricane of 1906. None of it seemed senseless or capricious to her: "Alas, it had to go; and so one thing after another had to be taken before this poor piece of humanity was fit for the Master's use, able to yield and to help others to yield. And now I thank the great Father for all that crushing and sorrow, as I used as a child to thank and adore my father for his punishments."

While her father's discipline, example, and spiritual presence were part of what sustained her, he himself remains, both in his letters and in her accounts of him, curiously anonymous, generic rather than specific. His interests were wide and judicious; his inner eye saw a neoclassical world—harmonious, hierarchical, lucid, and impersonal. It is hard to connect him to the incessant and demanding reality around him, to all the vexation, doubt, and fear that had made a martyr of his mother. The ricefields smelled to high heaven in summer, during the "long flow." His health was seldom good; each May his entire household had to be moved across Waccamaw Neck to Pawley's Island, to escape the endemic malaria. Slavery conditioned everything that he could permit himself to think, feel, or say. But through a kind of educated blindness, he was able to see only what he calls the planter's "regular and rational mode of life." His "Essay on Sea Coast Crops" was the definitive treatise on the cultivation of rice, and is impressively detailed. In it, Allston pauses briefly to celebrate the life of the planter:

> Bred in the country amid the exuberance of nature, in her just proportions and distributions, his mind is accustomed to her gradual processes, the regular succession of seasons and the annual recurrence of the routine of labor allotted by the Creator. His gifts acquire strength, character, and virtue. . . . In the creation around him, even of inanimate Nature,
>> He finds tongues in trees, books in running
>> brooks,
>> Sermons in stone, and good in everything.

No suggestion here of the mud, disease, and pervasive human degradation that surrounded him. Nature's proportions and distributions were just.

He was an earnest and energetic Episcopalian, humble before his God, but that humility too was part of the logic of the plantation: "The first element in the composition of one in authority," he writes his son Ben in 1860, "is to obey orders and conform to instructions notwithstanding the privations necessary." He oversaw, down to its last details of rations, clothing, tasks, rewards, and punishments, the operation of the plantation, and the plantation ratified, as the untidy democracy upriver did not, a fully articulated chain of being. It descended from Providence to him, through him to his family, through overseer, house servants, craftsmen, field hands (subdivided mathematically—full hands, half-hands, quarter-hands) to the infants, the sick, and the exhausted; from the house dogs to the hounds and horses, the mules, oxen, beeves, hogs, sheep, and chickens; the deer and turkey that haunted his woods and provided him sport; the ducks, coots, and bobolinks that fed upon his rice and upon which he and his dependents fed; the shad that swarmed up his rivers in late winter; the bass, bream, drum, sea-trout, and sailor's-choice; the shrimp, oyster, crab, and clam that varied and augmented the diet of master and slave.

He died in March of 1864, as Grant began the final, inexorable campaign against Richmond, and Sherman advanced on Atlanta. Within a year, his house would be ransacked and his people freed. In 1865, after Sherman had passed through, Jane Pringle, who was to become Elizabeth Allston's mother-in-law, wrote to Allston's widow: "Had I a place up the country I should have fled there gladly, [but] this is my only home and we cling to it with the blind tenacity of insects." Years later, Elizabeth commented on the cemetery at Chicora Wood, where Allston slaves had been buried for over a hundred years, and where their descendants continued to be buried:

> And still they come. It does not matter if they have died elsewhere
> if they are prosperous, and even if it is a mighty effort they beg to
> be brought "home" and laid by their people. As my father owned
> 600 of them when the war ended, it makes a number of funerals, for
> all the descendants of those want to be laid here. There is something
> very touching about it to me.

An ethos like R. F. Allston's appears to be a purely cultural construct, something that detached him from his circumstances

and justified his power over them. But an ethos may also be something more mysterious, a subtle awareness of place, a pervasive openness to the possibilities of purely local divinity. It must have been something like this that brought the former slaves back to Chicora to be buried, and Robert Allston probably had some feeling for it. But he could not speak of it; it was too "romantic," too unclear in its political and social tendencies, for him to acknowledge publicly. It would have been like admitting to a belief in ghosts. In one way or another, his daughter Elizabeth speaks of it in almost every paragraph she writes. She was her father's daughter, and sought to go on believing in the divine benevolence and orderliness of things, but she also possessed gifts that he apparently did not—a sense of humor, an ability to detach herself from her own station, and to identify herself with the dignity and feelings of any de facto human being she encountered. She did not cling to the old life and the old place with the blind tenacity of an insect, but with the resourcefulness of an artist who had found her vocation.

When Bishop came down the river in 1874, the plantation system appeared to have survived. Allstons were still planting rice; former slaves and their descendants still lived in the "streets," or quarters they had occupied before the war, and still worked the fields, either for wages or for a percentage of the crop. We can now see all this as only a temporary remission, but to the surviving Allstons, Pringles, and Westons, and to the hundreds of blacks bound by loyalty, ignorance, or necessity, this was simply life, as absorbing and demanding as it had ever been. When the Allston estate, hugely encumbered by debt, had finally been settled, Elizabeth's mother received, as her claim of dower, Chicora Wood, which had been the family's principal residence before the war. Elizabeth married Julian Pringle, and so became the mistress of White House, a few miles downstream from Chicora Wood. Like her mother and her grandmother, she was fated to a long widowhood, which left her to cope with an enormously complex operation without companionship or assistance.

It was possibly to her advantage that she was younger than either her mother or grandmother had been when widowed, but all other circumstances were against her. Rice was now being produced more cheaply elsewhere; capital was in shorter supply than ever; and, of course, the mutual dependency, mutual suspicion, and mutual antagonism of the two races had assumed a new form. Neither ex-slaves nor ex-slave-owners had the power to impose their wills, and neither could go it alone. In the upcountry, it was at least plausible to imagine that the plantations could be broken up, freedmen could be given forty acres and a mule, and cotton would still be produced. Rice could not be grown that way in the Carolina low country, any more than coal could be mined by individual miners working out of individual pits with their individual picks and shovels.

Here in late March, 80 or 100 or 150 years ago, planting would have been getting under way. Elizabeth Allston Pringle's formal education had prepared her to inhabit a Jane Austen novel, as education always prepares us to live in some more or less hypothetical environment. She was thoroughly grounded in French and Italian and music; her moral perceptions were refined; her delicacy was fostered. She might easily have played out the role of the displaced aristocrat, and spent her life lamenting the vulgar considerations that obtruded themselves upon her. But instead her education allowed her to see the strangeness and richness of her own world; she was both of it and not of it.

She describes the rice planting in the late spring of 1903. Normally it would have been in March, but planting that year had been severely delayed by big floods, and subsequent repair work on the dikes. It was nearly June before she could get the seed into the ground. One imagines the frustration of waiting on the water to come down, and the worry about money. Every year she in effect bet the plantation on the rice crop, and this year she was far behind even before she started. Yet she savored the rituals of planting: the preparation of the seed, which had to be coated with clay, so that it would not float to the surface when the fields were flooded; the transporting of seed, oxen, and a mechanical seeder by barge down to the field to be planted; the air of festivity and celebration that went with the sowing, and the beginning of a new cycle. She oversaw the work with an eye that was experienced but still impressionable:

> I went down into the marsh field, where five ploughs are running. . . . it is a 26 acre field, very level and pretty, and I am delighted with the work; it is beautiful. When I told one of the hands how pleased I was with the work, he said: "Miss, de lan' plough so sweet, we haf for to do'um good." I went through all with much pleasure, though I sank into the moist, dark brown soil too deep for comfort, and found it very fatiguing to jump the quarter drains, small ditches at a distance of 200 feet apart, and, worse, to walk the very narrow plank over the 10-foot ditch which runs all around the field and is very deep.
>
> The evening is beautiful; the sun, just sinking in a hazy, mellow light, is a fiery dark red, the air is fresh from the sea, only three miles to the east, the rice field banks are gay with flowers, white and blue violets, blackberry blossoms, wisteria, and the lovely blue jessamine, which is as sweet as an orange blossom. Near the bridge two negro women are fishing, with great strings of fish beside them.

She was at this time two years shy of her sixtieth birthday. She could take nothing for granted—not the weather, not her health, not the willingness of her ex-slaves to accept her authority. But her attachment to the life she lived and the place she lived it was unshakable and sustaining. The next year, in April, she went out to supervise the planting of alfalfa in an upland field, only to find that the ground had not been properly tilled. The seed were soaked and ready to go into the earth. By cajoling, scolding, and negotiating, she got Aphrodite, a young black woman with three children, the oldest one only three years old, to come and hoe the field. As Aphrodite hoed, Elizabeth Allston Pringle sat on a blanket beside the field and minded the children, at first with exasperation and then with growing pleasure. And, undoubtedly as a way to regain her equanimity, she wrote in her journal. Late in the afternoon, she was able to survey the day's work, both literary and agricultural, with tranquility:

I am quite ashamed of the frame of mind in which I began this, but I will not tear it up. What is written is written. After this episode everything looks so different, and now at 4:30 the four acres are planted. . . . Now I can look up and beyond the gray earth, and glory in the beauty of God's world. Half of the field was planted in oats in the winter and it is now splendid, an expanse of intense vivid color. The field, about twenty acres, is a slight elevation surrounded on three sides by a swamp, in which the variety of young green is wonderful. The cypress with its feathery fringe of pale grass green, the water oak with its tender yellow green, the hickory with its true pure green, and the maple with its gamut of pink up and down the scale—pale salmon, rose pink, then a brick-dusty pink, and here at last it rises into rich crimson. Here and there the poplar, with its flowerlike leaves, the black gum with its black tracery of downward turned branches all edged with tender gray green. It is too beautiful for words, and behind all, accenting and bringing out the light airy beauty, is the dark blue green of the solemn pine forest.

Her looking from the "gray earth"—the field which had cost such trouble and travail—to contemplate the "beauty of God's world" is, one might say, a conditioned response: her grandmother had professed to believe that all her tribulations were to ready her for "another world, which we are doomed to, and ought to prepare for," and her father's discipline had instilled the belief in her. But she was able to see and to live, and to experience the religious sentiment as a reality within the reality around her.

The reality around her included much that would give one pause—often enough, she encountered a moccasin under the steps or in the flower garden. She was isolated, day and night and for weeks on end, among a people whom she had to trust; there were adventures with runaway horses, with two black men whom she found stealing her timber, and a white hired man who promised to kill her when she rebuked him; there were hurricanes, floods, and fevers. And there were medical emergencies—a boy gets hold of a pistol and shoots himself in the hand; Wishy, a man living on the place, gets into a fight and his skull is fractured. She improvises and copes; Wishy survives:

> I dipped absorbent cotton in brandy and then into powdered alum, and put it into the hole in the top of Wishy's head; it seemed a gulf! I put in more and more, having Frank hold his hands closely around the top of the head; but still the blood flowed. Then I sprinkled the powdered alum over all thickly until there was only one little round hole just in the middle; I made a little ball of cotton and alum and pressed it down into the hole with my finger and it was done.

Her life from day to day seems much closer to Isak Dinesen in *Out of Africa* than to Scarlett O'Hara or any other stereotype of postbellum belledom.

She sustained her father's world more effectively than he himself could have done. Her brother Ben was eventually defeated; he left the ricelands to take orders in the Episcopal church. A few miles to the northeast, D. W. Jordan, having come down from the pinelands of the upper Waccamaw and bought Laurel Hill plantation, was trying hard to persuade himself that the old cornerstone of his Christian-rationalist faith—*Quinquid est, est rectum*—was unshaken by defeat, emancipation, and economic collapse, "but it is hard to yield our mind to what it teaches." Surveying the ruined world around him, he blamed the black man's sloth and improvidence, and seriously questioned whether such a creature had a soul: "I can hardly think he will go to the same heaven as the white man." Elizabeth Pringle's love for her birthplace survived all of this, and survived the temptations of embitterment. Her writing brought her a little income, and, although the rice culture was utterly dead by the beginnings of the First World War, she managed to hang onto Chicora Wood, and died there in 1922.

In late March of 1985, the cypress, oak, hickory, and black gum were much as she had described them, just coming into color. The ricefields are now all marshes; the quarter drains have filled in, but the larger ditches remain, as do many of the dikes. In most of the old fields, the tides come and go freely. The great openness of sky and marsh make the country seem bigger than it is, and the plantation houses are still spaced, at generous intervals, along the west bank. The names of the ones we passed, and of the others over on the Waccamaw side, often evoke the planters' visions of themselves—Arundel, Litchfield, Richmond Hill, Fairfield, Waterford, Nightingale Hall, and, most tellingly, Caledonia, Waverly, and Strawberry Hill. But others had nothing to do with Horace Walpole, Walter Scott, or romantic and baronial pretensions. Hasty Point was so named because Francis Marion had made a sudden and undignified escape from the British there during the Revolution; Tip Top was located at the uppermost upstream limit of rice planting; Forlorn Hope speaks for itself, and Pipe Down would appear to discourage delusions of grandeur.

When I was growing up, and even now, this country preserved its sense of being a world apart; entering it felt like entering a kingdom. Great wealth continues to command the high land and the marshes of the lower Pee Dee. With the final collapse of the planters, the plantations passed into the hands of rich sportsmen, who bought them for the duck-hunting in the marshes, and the quail-hunting in the pinelands, and who maintained the houses as lodges. Many of these people were Yankees, but many were not. The dream vision of a plantation haunts South Carolinians of a certain sort, and if a man made a pile of money, nothing in his heritage tempted him to buy a yacht or a bungalow in Bermuda or an apartment in Paris. He bought a plantation, as a way of alleviating the embarrassment of riches. Even without rice, the ricefields ate up money—dikes had to be maintained, the larger ditches kept open, small ponds established and stout gates erected. All of this was to attract ducks and repel poachers. And, if only one unscrupulous man decided to "bait" his fields—scatter corn in them—then everyone else had to follow suit, or that man would have every duck in the ricefields all to himself. Baiting was illegal, and was so routinely done that Daddy once observed that if a man managed to kill a duck legally in Georgetown County, it would be by virtue of a miracle, an accident, or a simple oversight.

Ricky and I had distant cousins who had briefly owned plantations on the Pee Dee, and we would occasionally be invited down to hunt. I remembered the drive down from Conway in the pre-dawn, the turning off the highway and into a long alley of live oaks, at the end of which the big house loomed up in the head-lights. If the occasion were fancy, there would be a heavy break-fast, much talk, men, guns, dogs, and then, still in the darkness, down to the river. Depending on the field we were assigned to hunt, there would be a run upstream or downstream, a turning off into one of the confusing myriad of creeks, and then from the creek into a gated ditch. Unlocking the gate from a small boat in the darkness, and pulling it open against the weight of the water was an awkward business, and one wanted to be quiet about it. Then there would be a paddle up a ditch or two, a dragging of the boat across a low mud dam into a small pond, which was almost certainly baited, and then, inside a blind at last, the coming of day. The tense waiting in the blind as the darkness thinned and slowly the great marsh revealed itself seemed to me to be a prelude to something I had been waiting for all my life, without knowing what it would be. Yet the actual hunting seldom came to much—there might be big flocks in the distance, and shots from an adjacent field, but we didn't often wind up with any ducks to show for our labors. The experience was much more an experience of place than it was the pursuit of a quarry, although without that strained expectancy of watching and hoping, the experience of the place would have been enormously diluted.

It seemed strange to be paddling through this country now, jumping an occasional summer duck or small flock of blue-winged teal, and to be so utterly without urgency or anticipation of any sort. We passed Chicora Wood about mid-morning. The house was being restored—the roof re-shingled, new siding on the ell, the trim all bright and gleaming. A tasteful and unobtrusive tennis court had been installed, down beside the river. "No shortage of money there," Ricky said. And that indeed appeared to be the case at each of the plantations we passed. The old houses were no longer hunting lodges, but had become regular residences once again, for people who would never need to wade through the muck or leap a quarter drain. There was a lot of ricefield improvement going on as well, all of it for the benefit of ducks.

Just below Chicora Wood, Chapel Creek gives off to the west, and, as we were not pressed for time, we turned up it. The tide was high; when we got to the bridge where the river road crosses the creek, there wasn't enough clearance for us to go under. This mildly disappointed me—I remembered the upper part of the creek as a hushed, mysterious place, with trees hanging over the brown, sluggish stream, and creating a stillness so profound that you tended to speak in whispers, as though you were in a church. But Chapel Creek did not get its name from any innate sanctity. Just to the

south of it stood Prince Frederick's Chapel, which had been the central place of worship for the lords of the Pee Dee ricefields, their families, and at least some of their slaves.

I wanted to have a look at Prince Frederick's Chapel. Ricky volunteered to stay with the canoe. I walked a half-mile or so of perfectly flat and uncannily empty road, which ran as straight as a string ahead of me; I could look down it until the parallels of its margins and its center line converged, and it disappeared into an illusory infinity. If moving down the road toward its low, unchanging horizon, which never got any closer, had something of the feeling of moving inside an optical illusion, that impression was heightened when suddenly a clearing, invisible until I came abreast of it, opened on the left, and I confronted Prince Frederick's Chapel. It sits among weeds on sandy soil, and all that remains of it is the doorway, the bell tower, and the west facade. Nave, chancel, and everything else have gone, but it takes a moment to realize this, because you are looking at the building from a perspective which would not allow you a view of the whole building even if the whole building were there. The doorway is empty, and you look through it and see, not the twilit sanctuary of an ecclesiastical interior, but simply the same sunlit ordinariness that surrounds you.

The chapel is made of plastered-over brick, and is neo-Romanesque in style. It had once been an impressive building. Services were still occasionally held in it during my childhood, but by then it was already a church without a parish, and had to import its congregation from Conway and Georgetown. The diocese had finally conceded to demography, and the church had been abandoned to the Lord, and to the nature that is now reclaiming it. A small sweetgum has managed to root itself on top of the bell tower. It will die there, but not before its roots have opened up new ways for the weather to work its way in, and undermine what little is left. The shutters in the belfry windows are broken; a phoebe had built a nest between the slats of one of them. Inside, on the beam that had sustained the bells, barn swallows have made themselves at home, and everywhere on the exposed lathe and the framing behind the lathe are the hard little conical nests of dirt daubers.

The plantation South always held a nostalgic vision of itself as a society that was agrarian, traditional, deeply rooted in some unfallen age of faith. If slavery could be conceived of as a kind of modification and continuation of feudalism, an ancient and stable pattern of social and economic relationships, then the raw reality of it might be blurred, if not altogether effaced. The church was a necessary part of this nostalgia. It asserted a sacred hierarchy, authorizing and redeeming the life of servitude. Looking at Prince Frederick's, you fall easily into a kind of sentimental reverie, and see in your mind's eye black and white men and women filing decorously through the arched door, or restive horses snuffling and stamping under a big oak as the service droned on, Sunday in and Sunday out, generation after generation.

But the reality of Prince Frederick's was quite different. Elizabeth Pringle describes her father's final trip there, in the March of 1864:

> He was laid to rest in the churchyard of Prince Frederick's, just a mile away [from Chicora Wood], where the beautiful half-finished brick church in whose building he had been so much interested, stood, a monument to war. All the trimmings and furnishings had been ordered in England, and, in running the blockade, they had been sunk. The architect, whose name was Gunn, had died, and was buried near the church, and the beautiful but roofless building stood there forlorn. There we laid him, with all the beauty of the wild spring flowers and growth he so loved around him, nearly under a big dogwood tree in all its white glory. Crying and lamentation of the negroes who flocked along the road behind the wagon which carried Papa, and [who] filled the large graveyard, standing at a little distance behind the family, according to their rank and station on the plantation. Those who dug the grave had been specially named by Papa, and it was considered a great honor.

And so the church which I had always considered ancient had not in fact been completed before the Civil War. Like so many things about the antebellum South, it became complete only as a memory, and stood for its surprisingly brief life as a shrine where a living world worshipped an idea that had never been realized, and now was dead.

I walked out into the churchyard behind the ruin. No one had maintained it; many of the stones were knocked over or broken off. Lower South Carolina is said to resemble China, in that its citizens eat rice and worship their ancestors, but no one in the land of the living was paying any homage to these illustrious dead. The great names were here—Weston and Allston and Sparkman—but I have never seen this kind of complete abandonment in even the poorest sort of country churchyard in Horry County, where the all but anonymous folk who lived in ragged cabins and eked out a mean living lie in graves that may be marked with nothing more than cypress headboards or shards of colored glass. In Horry, it was simply a matter of continuity—people went on living and worshipping in the same places. Until recently, history gave them little, and, until recently, history took little from them. That wasn't the case here in the ricelands.

The one living thing I found was a dainty little moccasin, at the back edge of the churchyard. I saw him in plenty of time and stopped. He coiled tighter into himself and hissed, showing the shockingly white, silky inner lining of his mouth. I considered killing him, but didn't, for more or less literary reasons:

> They say the Lion and the Lizard keep
> The Courts where Jamshy'd gloried and drank deep.

This was South Carolina, where we had no lions, and churchyards instead of courtyards, but the moccasin belonged here, as an index of oblivion. We watched each other for a while, and then he uncoiled and flowed away, in that strangely stately way of a snake.

When I returned to the bridge and the canoe, we decided to go ahead and have lunch there. As we were eating, a black man came walking up from the direction of Chicora Wood, with his own lunch neatly wrapped in wax paper. He was tall, past middle age, and spoke with a pleasing deliberation. He told us he had been replacing some slats in one section of the picket fence that separates Chicora Wood from the highway, and was taking his lunch break. We fell into conversation, and I was pleased to learn that you could still catch a mess of bonnet bream in the upper part of Chapel Creek on falling water. We asked him who owned Chicora Wood now, and he said the man's name, which was altogether unfamiliar. "He come from somewhere else, California or

Colorado, I believe," he said, pronouncing the two places syllable by syllable—Cally FORN ya; Colly RA do—as though to emphasize their outlandishness. We asked him about other plantations, upriver and down, and he seemed to have done carpentry work or house painting at almost all of them, and could tell us who their current and recent owners were. "They some rich men be living on this river," he said, "but this California man, he's *oilfield* money. Tell me he could take 'im others like this," and he tore off a piece of bread from his sandwich and rolled it into a pellet, "and do 'im like this," and he popped the pellet into his mouth and swallowed it without chewing, the way a toad swallows a fly.

Ricky said that we'd noticed a lot of work going on at Chicora Wood, and he nodded emphatically: "He doing it *right*. Tell me he found a old woman used to work in that house when old Miz Pringle there—old black woman from Georgetown and blind as a bat. But he take her up to the house and she walk 'round inside it, feelin' the walls and feelin' the doors and the moldings and ever-'ting. Anyting different, she tell 'im: 'This ain't right; it wurn't like this.' And they say that old woman picture it all in her mind, right the way ever'ting was, and she tell 'im about it, and he put it all back that way."

We finished lunch. He asked us where we were headed and we said Georgetown. He pointed to Chapel Creek. While we were eating the tide had slacked and now the water, in a motion as silent and stealthy as the motion of respiration in an animal, had begun to ebb back toward the Pee Dee. By the time we regained the river, the tide would be running strongly. "You won't have no trouble reaching Georgetown for supper," he said. We said goodbye and left him sitting on the bridge railing in the warm spring sun.

As we paddled back down Chapel Creek, I thought of the restoration job going on at Chicora Wood. I did not doubt that it would be scrupulous, and that, like any scrupulous restoration, it would abstract the past from all its contingencies and makeshift improvisations. What would Elizabeth Pringle have made of it? Plantation houses in her time were places of incessant practical activity; for all their pretensions to manorial style, they were also farmhouses, on a very large scale, and, like any farmhouse, they were seldom spic and span—patched and peeling would be more like it. Gilmore had found it ironic that, in the heart of the turpentine country, most of the fine residences he saw were in great need of a coat of paint.

In the long years when she inhabited the house as a solitary widow of very limited means, Elizabeth Pringle accepted, and seems to have cherished, the ravages of nature. She describes her peacock:

> The dear departed peacock, whose mate was eaten up by a fox while sitting on a nest of beautiful eggs, lived three years in a state of single misery, during which time he broke every pane of glass in the windows he could reach. It was so pathetic that I could not give way to wrath and have him beaten away. He was looking for that lovely mate, with her graceful long neck and dainty small head, and seemed to think she was imprisoned in the house, for he roamed round and round it . . . and when, peering in through the window glass, he caught sight of his own iridescent form, he would plunge forward in an ecstasy of joy, break the glass, cut his poor, proud head, and hastily fly away, only to begin the search again as soon as his wounds were healed. In this way the windows were broken one by one, and the dirt daubers (a very busy flying thing that looks exactly like a wasp, but does not sting) came in and made their wonderful clay nests in the halls, so that it looked like some old, deserted, haunted place.

She was unable to replace all of the panes, some of which had "a pointed arched top like a church window, and that shape of glass I could not get," and so the dirt daubers had run of the hallway for years, until she finally obtained some screening and shut them out.

The peacock continued to haunt the house:

He reminded me of that tragic scene in Gluck's *Orpheus and Eurydice*, when he dares to enter the vast terrible kingdom of the dead in his search for his beloved—the eager, pathetic gaze into the lifeless face of each veiled form, the joy of imagined recognition, only to fade into disappointment and horror as returning life shows the mistaken identity. Occasionally he would go into the busy poultry yard and spread out his beautiful fan and salaam to the white Leghorn hens and win their cackling admiration, but these exhibitions became rarer each year, and finally he disappeared. I am quite sure he sought the solitude of the forest to die.

The new owners would not restore the dirt daubers and the peacock, and, more importantly, they were unlikely to have Elizabeth Pringle's imaginative sympathy with a world of life so disrespectful of private property. Her sensibility was in some ways high-flown and romantic—from what I know of barnyards, I expect the peacock saw its image as a rival to be assaulted, and not a peahen-Eurydice to be rescued—and yet it connected her to all the life around her. Whatever else her peacock is, as it stalks around the house haunted by memories and delusions, it is not a self-portrait. She sees the humor as well as the sadness of its situation, and keeps her balance, not allowing pity to become self-pity. I imagined that life at Chicora Wood now might turn out to be grander, duller, and, in a special sense, more isolated, than it had been for her. A few dark blue dirt daubers, flickering about their domestic routines, wouldn't be a bad addition.

And now we left Chicora Wood behind. Near the mouth of Chapel Creek, a red-shouldered hawk wheeled into sight above us, hung for a moment, and suddenly folded up and went into a steep dive. He fell so fast that the whole bird seemed to ripple and flex, the way a paper kite does when it is streaming out of control toward earth. He passed below the treetops and out of our sight; I half expected to hear a crash or detonation of the hawk hitting the ground. But in a few seconds he came back into sight, out over the marshes across the river, riding the momentum

of his plunge up to another crest, holding there for another moment and crying out his blue jay's cry, then collapsing into another exuberant stoop. I supposed it was some sort of prenuptial display; Ricky said he didn't know how it might impress another hawk, but it impressed the hell out of him.

We continued down past Dirlington Plantation and Nightingale Hall, losing more and more of the Pee Dee to the Waccamaw as we went. Below Nightingale, the marshes spread out on both sides of the river; the high land to the west is visible only as a distant tree line. To the east, there is only an occasional solitary cypress or gum, rooted on an old dike, to stand out against the immensity of sky and marsh. The sea breeze, coming up from the south, reached us here, and carried with it the first faint smell of salt marsh and salt mud. It also brought some sudden dark clouds, and by the time we reached the mouth of the Pee Dee, and looked out onto the wide, flat expanse of Winyah Bay, there was a hard little squall of wind and rain—coming toward us, it ripped and silvered the surface of the Bay like a school of fish. We dropped to our knees—Ricky was in the stern now—and lowered our heads the way a jogger might when a big truck roars by on the highway, and paddled hard. And just about managed to hold our ground until, in a matter of two or three minutes, the weather passed us by, leaving in its wake the freshness of rain to mingle with the salt smell of the sea. A string of ibis came over, flying upriver, a solitary anhinga, looking like somebody who was trying to catch up to a bus, followed them, flapping and then soaring a few yards, in a wobbling, unsteady way.

U.S. 17 crosses the Bay on a long, low bridge that arches up in the center to permit navigation. We were not navigation, and hung close along the western shore, out of the whitecaps created between the sea wind and the falling tide. Once we were under the bridge, Georgetown came into sight—a low town dominated by two towering smokestacks. One of these belonged to the International Paper Company, and a plume of windblown smoke carried from it over the town and across the Bay in a slowly unravelling scarf a mile long. The other belonged to a German steel-manufacturing firm that had established itself here about a decade ago. It had been the familiar story—a town desperately in need of jobs and taxes, a company that agreed to various conditions pertaining to air quality, environmental impact, and so forth. Then the perfectly predictable unanticipated difficulties and expenses with construction, the absolute necessity that the town relax its restrictions if the plant were to be finished at all, the mutual recriminations and inevitable triumph of economic logic, and now what we saw—a brownish haze that seemed to emanate from the whole factory, and not just from its smokestack, and that gave a sepia tint to a considerable portion of the Georgetown skyline.

We paddled past a yacht basin that, as Ricky observed with a sniff, no self-respecting canoeist would deign to use, and turned up into the Sampit River, a short tidal stream that empties into the Bay on the south side of Georgetown. Here there was an inelegant, working waterfront—heaps of bleached oyster shells, creosoted pilings streaked with gull shit, and trawlers snugged in tight against their wharves. We slipped under the stern of a big shrimper, and into an informal landing of shell, mud, and sand. The trip was over.

Ricky walked up into Georgetown. We had left my truck in the yard of Mrs. Norma Sellars. Twenty years ago, when he taught at Winyah High School, she had been his landlady, and, by mutual and implied consent, she had become a kind of honorary aunt to him—they had kept in touch through all his wanderings, and he visited her whenever a pretext presented itself. I had just finished unloading the canoe and bringing everything out to the road when he came rattling up in the truck. We loaded it, tied down the canoe, and returned to Mrs. Sellar's—she'd told Ricky to go get me and come back for tea.

Her house was on a quiet street—a small, tight old cape-styled house that would have been at home in Maine or Massachusetts, and that had in fact been built by a transplanted Yankee not long after the Revolution. We sat in her snug, low parlor and had tea and talked. She was a tall, big-boned, and downright woman, somewhere in her seventies, I judged, with a bright eye and a quick, soft laugh. We talked about the river and the ricefields; she'd visited most of the plantations at one time or another. I mentioned how visible the smoke and haze were when you approached Georgetown from the water, and she laughed and said that she didn't need to see it, she could smell it; anybody that lived in Georgetown knew what money smelled like. And there was a lot of money around now—fine new houses going up in North Georgetown and across the Bay, over on Waccamaw Neck. But it was a pity in a way. Back then—she made a gesture with her hand that annihilated decades—nobody in Georgetown County had had any money and there was beautiful land, beautiful places to build. Now some people had plenty of money and built big fancy houses, but just built them all in a row, where they didn't have much to look at except each other.

She asked Ricky how he liked being back in Conway, and he

said not much—the house was all right, but he wished there was some chance of getting into the country, where he could have a big garden and maybe a horse or some chickens. He seemed able to talk to her candidly, and said he wasn't sure whether he could stay on in South Carolina, with so many people moving in and so little space left to knock around in. She smiled at him. "You're the way my Daddy was," she said. "When I was little he told me, 'Norma, whether you build a house or buy a house, remember, there's three things you got to consider.'" She paused a second, to allow us to anticipate what it was her father had said, and then she told us: " 'Location.' " she said, holding her index finger aloft and touching her thumb to it, then raising the next two fingers in turn and counting them off: " 'Location. And location.' "

# Notes

PAGE

7  John Thomas, "Slavery in the Horry District in the Mid-Nineteenth Century," *The Independent Republic Quarterly* (Horry County Historical Society; hereafter cited as *IRQ*) (Fall 1982).

7  *Myrtle Beach Area Report*, comp. Karen Dover, publicity brochure (Greensboro, S.C.: Fisher-Harrison Quality of Life Publications), p. 71.

11  A. Goff Bedford, *The Independent Republic* (Privately published, 1985), p. 6.

13  Kathryne Smith Hurt, "Some Facts About the Descendants of James Smith, Sr., of Horry County, S.C.," *IRQ* (Spring 1983).

14  Frances Ann Kemble, *Journal of a Residence on a Georgia Plantation*, ed. John A. Scott (New York, 1975), p. 35.

15–17  Edmund Kirke (pseud. for James Robert Gilmore), *Among the Pines, or the South in Secession Time* (New York, 1862), passim.

18  George Eliot, *Works*, vol. 15 (Boston, 1900), pp. 19–20.

19  W. M. Teller, ed., *On the River* (New Brunswick, N.J.: Rutgers University Press, 1976), p. 52.

26–27  John Bartram, *Diary of a Journey Through the Carolinas, Georgia, and Florida, from July 1, 1765 to April 10, 1766*, Transactions of the American Philosophical Society, n.s. 33, no. 1 (Philadelphia, 1942), p. 16;

William Bartram, *Travels of William Bartram*, ed. Mark Van Doren (New York, 1940), p. 374.

46 Nathaniel Holmes Bishop, *The Voyage of the Paper Canoe* (New York, 1878), pp. 217–218.

50 Ibid., p. 223.

67 On the turpentining industry in the Waccamaw basin, see Charles W. Joyner, "The Far Side of the Forest: Timber and Naval Stores in the Waccamaw Region," *IRQ* (Fall 1984).

68 James Craigie, "Crossing the River at Wortham's Ferry," *IRQ* (Spring 1980).

75 Bishop, p. 231.

85–86 Ibid., pp. 233–234.

97 Ibid., p. 237.

105–106 *IRQ* (Winter 1981), reprints a memoir-letter written by Lucille Godfrey to her grandson, Samuel Godfrey Dargan. In a few instances, my memory of the stories she used to tell me varies from what she writes here. In such cases, I have given my version rather than hers, although hers is obviously the more accurate. I am shocked to learn, for example, that the owner of the Horse That Wasn't Afraid of Trains was not my grandfather at all. The lore of family history, like other forms of gossip, is obviously modified, synthesized, and fitted to preconceptions and to the demands of a good story in the process of transmission. As a child, I believed in the past only as a story, and the story I believed is what I want to convey here.

108–112 Elizabeth Collins, *Memories of the Southern States* (Tauton, 1865), passim. I am indebted to the staff of the Boston Athenaeum for allowing me to sit in a stately, high-ceilinged room on a snowy winter morning, and read this strange little book about Horry and Snow Hill.

116–118 Arthur Middleton Manigault, *A Carolinian Goes to War: Memoirs of General Arthur Middleton Manigault*, ed. R. Lockwood Tower (Columbia: University of South Carolina Press, 1983), pp. 77–78, et passim.

121 Franklin G. Burroughs, "Snow Hill," *IRQ* (Spring 1981).

155 Eugenia Buck Cutts, "Formation of the Communities of Bucksport and Bucksville," *IRQ* (Fall 1980); "The Cutts-Pendleton Correspondence," *IRQ* (Fall 1976).

PAGE

178  Bishop, p. 240.

179  *The South Carolina Rice Plantation as Revealed in the Papers of Robert F. W. Allston,* ed. J. H. Easterby (Chicago, 1945), p. 54.

180  Joyner, passim, for a detailed account of rice cultivation and slave culture in the Georgetown District.

181  Elizabeth W. Allston Pringle, *Chronicles of Chicora Wood* (New York, 1922), p. 110.

182  Ibid., p. 118.

183  Quoted in Patience Pennington (pseud. for Elizabeth W. Allston Pringle), *A Woman Rice Planter,* ed. C. O. Cathey (Cambridge, Mass.: 1961), p. xxviii; *South Carolina Rice Plantation,* p. 210.

185–186  *A Woman Rice Planter,* p. 386.

186  Ibid., pp. 12–13.

187  Ibid., pp. 166–167.

188  Ibid., pp. 17–18.

189  "The Diary of Colonel Daniel W. Jordan," *IRQ* (Spring 1981).

194  Pringle, *Chronicles of Chicora Wood,* p. 209.

197–198  *A Woman Rice Planter,* pp. 415–417.

# Selected Bibliography

Bartram, John. *Diary of a Journey Through the Carolinas, Georgia, and Florida, from July 1, 1765 to April 10, 1766.* Transactions of the American Philosophical Society. New series. Vol. 33, no. 1. Philadelphia, 1942.

Bartram, William. *Travels of William Bartram.* Edited by Mark Van Doren. New York, 1940.

Bedford, A. Goff. *The Independent Republic.* Privately published, 1985.

Bishop, Nathaniel Holmes. *The Voyage of the Paper Canoe.* New York, 1878.

Burroughs, Franklin. "Snow Hill." *Independent Republic Quarterly* (Spring 1981).

Collins, Elizabeth. *Memories of the Southern States.* Tauton, 1865.

Craigie, James. "Crossing the River at Wortham's Ferry." *Independent Republic Quarterly* (Spring 1980).

Cutts, Eugenia Buck. "The Cutts-Pendleton Correspondence." *Independent Republic Quarterly* (Fall 1976).

————. "Formation of the Communities of Bucksport and Bucksville." *Independent Republic Quarterly* (Fall 1980).

"The Diary of Colonel Daniel W. Jordan." *Independent Republic Quarterly* (Spring 1981).

Godfrey, Lucille, to her grandson Samuel Godfrey Dargan. *Independent Republic Quarterly* (Winter 1981).

Hurt, Kathryne Smith. "Some Facts About the Descendants of James Smith, Sr." *Independent Republic Quarterly* (Spring 1983).

*Independent Republic Quarterly.* Published by the Horry County Historical Society, Conway, South Carolina.

Joyner, Charles W. *Down by the Riverside.* Columbia: University of South Carolina Press, 1984.

————. "The Far Side of the Froest: Timber and Naval Stores in the Waccamaw Region." *Independent Republic Quarterly* (Fall 1984).

Kemble, Frances Ann. *Journal of a Residence on a Georgia Plantation.* Edited by John A. Scott. New York, 1975.

Kirke, Edmund (pseud. for James Robert Gilmore). *Among the Pines, or the South in Secession Time.* New York, 1862.

Manigault, Arthur Middleton. *A Carolinian Goes to War: Memoirs of General Arthur Middleton Manigault.* Edited by R. Lockwood Tower. Columbia: University of South Carolina Press, 1983.

*Myrtle Beach Area Report.* Compiled by Karen Dover. Publicity brochure from Fisher-Harrison Quality of Life Publications, Greensboro, South Carolina.

Pennington, Patience (pseud. for Elizabeth W. Allston Pringle). *A Woman Rice Planter.* Edited by C. O. Cathey. Cambridge, Mass., 1961.

Pringle, Elizabeth W. Allston. *Chronicles of Chicora Wood.* New York, 1922.

*The South Carolina Rice Plantation as Revealed in the Papers of Robert F. W. Allston.* Edited by J. H. Easterby. Chicago, 1945.

Teller, W. M., ed. *On the River.* New Brunswick, N.J.: Rutgers University Press, 1976.

Thomas, John. "Slavery in the Horry District in the Mid-Nineteenth Century." *Independent Republic Quarterly* (Fall 1982).